Enterprise Content Management, Records Management and Information Culture Amidst e-Government Development

Chandos
Information Professional Series
Series Editor: Ruth Rikowski
(email: Rikowskigr@aol.com)

Chandos' new series of books is aimed at the busy information professional. They have been specially commissioned to provide the reader with an authoritative view of current thinking. They are designed to provide easy-to-read and (most importantly) practical coverage of topics that are of interest to librarians and other information professionals. If you would like a full listing of current and forthcoming titles, please visit www.chandospublishing.com.

New authors: we are always pleased to receive ideas for new titles; if you would like to write a book for Chandos, please contact Dr Glyn Jones on g.jones.2@elsevier.com or telephone +44 (0) 1865 843000.

Enterprise Content Management, Records Management and Information Culture Amidst e-Government Development

Proscovia Svärd

ELSEVIER

CP
CHANDOS
PUBLISHING
An imprint of Elsevier • elsevier.com

Chandos Publishing is an imprint of Elsevier
50 Hampshire Street, 5th Floor, Cambridge, MA 02139, United States
The Boulevard, Langford Lane, Kidlington, OX5 1GB, United Kingdom

British Library Cataloguing-in-Publication Data
A catalogue record for this book is available from the British Library

Library of Congress Cataloging-in-Publication Data
A catalog record for this book is available from the Library of Congress

ISBN: 978-0-08-100874-4 (print)
ISBN: 978-0-08-100900-0 (online)

For information on all Chandos Publishing
visit our website at https://www.elsevier.com/books-and-journals

Publisher: Glyn Jones
Acquisition Editor: George Knott
Editorial Project Manager: Charlotte Rowley
Senior Production Project Manager: Priya Kumaraguruparan
Cover designer: Mark Rogers

Contents

Acknowledgments

This book is based on my PhD research and it would not have been possible if it was not for funding that I received during my PhD process. I would therefore like to acknowledge the following institutions: the Centre for Digital Information Management (CEDIF) at Mid Sweden University that received the European Union Objective 2 funding and where I carried out my Licentiate research, the University of Amsterdam, Faculty of Humanities where I completed my PhD, and lastly, the School of Interdisciplinary Research and Post-Graduate Studies, University of South Africa where I have been as a Postdoctoral Research Fellow—2016–17. Without the postdoctoral research position, it would have been difficult to engage in writing. I would also like to thank my husband Anders Rickard Svärd and my children Felicia Mona Svärd and Kevin Rickard Svärd that always bear with me and continue to be my support-system.

Introduction

Scope and audience

This book has been inspired by my work in government institutions, teaching at universities, and research experiences. The book, therefore, draws on both my licentiate and PhD theses and discusses the impact e-Government development has had on information management, presents the concepts of Enterprise Content Management (ECM), Records Management (RM), Information Culture, and the Records Continuum Model (RCM). A lot is going on in the information management field and we are witnessing different kinds of information management constructs promising to deliver the magic bullet to the challenges posed by digital information. There seems to be a realization that information is a vital resource that should be effectively managed for successful business. Despite this awareness and the fact that most people in organizations today are information creators, information responsibilities are left to IT departments, archivists, and records managers. My own work experience confirmed that very few people in my organization understood the challenges posed by the management of the information they produced or used in their work processes. The current digital information landscape requires competencies from an array of disciplines, such as information architects, records managers, the business people, archivists, lawyers, business analysts, and IT personnel. Everybody has to be involved if information management is to be integrated with the business processes and used to its maximum potential. This book, therefore, should be of interest to the different professions engaged in the management of digital information.

In theory, there are best practice standards to facilitate the management of information, but in practice, the challenges have become more complex. e-Government development has led to the development of integrated electronic services and also increased the amount of information that has to be managed. This also requires that the ownership of the information in such services is identified in order to establish who is responsible for its management. Though governments are promoting free access to information, quality information hinges on robust information management regimes, an information infrastructure with well-integrated systems and a culture that appreciates information as a vital resource. The book therefore discusses the impact e-Government development has had on information management and highlights the differences and similarities between ECM and RM. It further discusses the need to address the people issues, which are manifested in the type of information culture organizations embrace. It considers the use of the RCM as a model that promotes a proactive approach to the management of digital information and the pluralization of information as per the Public Sector Information (PSI) directive.

Structure of the book

The book constitutes seven chapters. Chapter 1 discusses the impact e-Government development has had on information management. The Public Sector Information Directive obliges European governments to avail government information to the citizens. Information is seen as a national resource that should boost the development of new electronic services and innovation. e-Government development further aims to increase accountability and transparency through the free flow of information. However, this will also require a robust information management infrastructure to facilitate the creation, capture, management, and pluralization of quality information.

Chapter 2 examines the concept of ECM as an emerging information management strategy and a field that is promoted by its proponents as the panacea to the challenges of digital information management since it enables enterprise-wide information management. It focuses on the management of both structured and unstructured content in an organization. It is a term used to cover a broad range of digital assets, including web content management, document management, and content management.

Chapter 3 focuses Records Management, which is an established field of practice that facilitates the management and maintenance of authentic, reliable, and complete records in societies. Good information and records management practices promote effective business processes and transparent and accountable governments.

Chapter 4 examines the two principles that govern the management of records; the Life Cycle Model and the Records Continuum Model. The Life Cycle Model applies the analogy of living organisms and presumes that records are born, live, and die. This is achieved through the phases of current, semicurrent, and non current where records should either be retained or disposed of. It is regarded insufficient in the digital environment. The RCM constitutes four dimensions, create, capture, organize, and pluralize, and combines the activities of managing both archival and current records. The RCM suits the current digital environment because it views information as always in the process of becoming. The model, therefore, promotes the repurposing of information than storage. The RCM through its pluralization dimension expects information to be used in different environments and by different stakeholders. This is also in line with for example the European Union Directive on the reuse of public information for innovative purposes.

Chapter 5 focuses on the differences and similarities between ECM and RM that were identified during the pursuit of my PhD research. The research that I carried out in two Swedish municipalities and the literature review that I undertook on ECM and RM facilitated an understanding of the two information management constructs.

Chapter 6 discusses the concept of information culture and the impact it has on the creation, management, and use of information in organizations. Good information and records management practices promote effective business processes. The information culture of an organization consists of attitudes and norms towards information and the way employees value it. This determines the management of information/records for accountability and transparency and for the execution of business processes. An organization has a mature information culture when it can easily access and use and uses information in its everyday activities. Organizations are populated by people with attitudes and behaviors that shape the success or failure of records and information management programs. The chapter uses case studies from Sweden and Belgium municipalities to demonstrate how information culture affects the management of public records and information.

Chapter 7 examines the concept of accountability and transparency and demonstrates why information management and information access are of key importance to social, cultural, and economic development. The free flow of government information enhances the democratic rights of the citizens. The only way citizens can hold those they vote into power accountable for the decisions they make on their behalf is through access to government information. Despite multistakeholder initiatives to promote accountability and transparency, there are many citizens of the world that are still governed by nontransparent and nonaccountable governments. There is still lack of empirical evidence on the impact of transparency and accountability initiatives on societies.

Proscovia Svärd

e-Government development and its impact on information management

1

1.1 e-Government development

e-Government development is now a global phenomenon and governments are investing in the transformation of the way their institutions operate, to make them more cost effective so that they can deliver efficient services to the citizens. e-Government is driven by policy goals of increased effectiveness, efficiency, information quality, improved interaction mechanisms, and in turn better governance tools. It aims to improve the performance of government institutions and has at its core the use of information technology and information. Scholl (2006) postulated that e-Government is a redefinition of information management in government with a strong institutional impact. It also means change in the way public authorities deliver services to the citizens and a redesign of ordinary ways of doing business. e-Government is therefore transformative in nature and affects the management of human, technological, and organization resources and processes (Grant & Chau, 2006). Archmann and Iglesias (2010) argued that e-Government requires thinking organizations, a change in processes and behavior. e-Government is defined by Layne & Lee, 2001 (p. 123) as the "government's use of technology, particularly web-based Internet applications to enhance the access to and delivery of government information and service to citizens, business partners, employees, other agencies, and government entities." Fang (2002) defined e-Government as "as a way for governments to use the most innovative information and communication technologies, particularly web-based Internet applications, to provide citizens and businesses with more convenient access to government information and services, to improve the quality of the services and to provide greater opportunities to participate in democratic institutions and processes." Nordfors, Ericson, and Lindell (2016) postulate that e-Government links services, information and dialogue. e-Government initiatives have meant the use of web-based technologies to disseminate information to the citizens and hence, a two-way communication flow that has been established (Richard 1999; Worall, 2010). e-Government has therefore affected the information management landscape. This is a domain where the societal and political aims intertwine with the progress of information technology.

Democratic developments take place when there is an effective flow of information between the government and its citizens (Yong, 2004). European governments are, e.g., encouraged to develop e-Government in order to establish a common

Enterprise Content Management, Records Management and Information Culture Amidst e-Government Development.
DOI: http://dx.doi.org/10.1016/B978-0-08-100874-4.00001-6

framework where technologies can be deployed to expand services, increase transparency, efficiency, and inclusion (United Nations Department of Economic and Social Affairs, 2012). The European e-Government Action Plan 2011–2015 promoted transparency and the reuse of data through the Public Sector Information Directive. The aim was to encourage the reuse of government information in order to produce new services but also to create more transparent decision making processes (The European Union, 2003). Governments around the world are promoting free access to government information. In the information society that we are all part of today, information is considered a major asset and vehicle for economic, cultural, and political achievements, enhanced by the use of information technology. Freedoms of expression and access to information are now cornerstones of modern democracies. Information is regarded as the oxygen of democracy and hence a promoter of good governance. Freedom of information (FOI) is underpinned by maximum disclosure and if information access is denied, there should be justification as to why (Article 19, 2002). Transparency is meant to create increased legitimacy, democratic participation, and trust in government institutions. Therefore, the principles of FOI laws include: transparency, accountability, public participation, and information to citizens (Worthy, 2010). The importance of the right to access information held by public bodies, sometimes referred to as the right to know, has e.g., existed in Sweden for over 200 years (Mendel, 2008).

Another aspect related to FOI laws that is not often discussed is the sustainability of long-term transparency. Jaeger and Bertot (2010) argued that the sustainability of long-term transparency requires that citizens can access the information that they seek regardless of format. The current digital environment has meant that governments disseminate information through social media and internet enabled technologies. This has long-term implications especially where the management of information is not proactively planned for. Therefore, governments need to put in place strategies that would allow long-term access to government information. The challenges of managing and preserving digital information over time are well known and call for enormous resources and a proactive approach (Bearman, 1994; Dollar, 2000; Duranti & Preston, 2008).

1.2 The public sector information directive

The implementation of e-Government has led to an increase in information and especially digitally born information, which puts new demands on information and records management practices (The International Records Management Trust, 2004). Central to transparent government is access to information by the general public and the media (Bohlin, 2010; Regeringskansliet, 2009). It is argued in the European Access to Official Documents Guide that: "The basic principle is that a broad right of access to official documents should be granted on the basis of equality and in application of clear rules, whilst refusal of access should be the exception and must be duly justified. It is not a question of recognizing merely the freedom of the public to have access to information which the authorities wish to give them, but rather to secure a genuine 'right to know' for the public. States must ensure, with due regard for certain rules, that anyone may, upon request, have access to documents held by public authorities" (Directorate General of Human Rights, 2004, p. 6). Therefore, one of the most important instruments of citizens' control of public authorities is the principle of public access to government information.

As government institutions engage in e-Government development and hence use information technology, they are generating lots of information hereto referred to as the Public Sector Information (PSI). The United Kingdom's Office of Public Sector Information stated that, "Information, particularly PSI, is at the head of the citizen's relationship with government and the public sector" (Office of Public Sector Information, 2009, p. 18). Government information is currently looked upon as a "gold mine" that should be explored by various stakeholders to boost national development through the creation of electronic services. The PSI is regulated by the European PSI Directive on repurposing of public information that was enacted in December 2003 and was to be implemented in the member states by July 2005. The Directive focuses on the economic aspects of public information reuse (European Union, 2003). For example, Fornefeld, Boele-Keimer, Recher, and Fanning (2009) argued that in most European public administrations making information available to the private sector is an indication of a cultural change. They further argued that previously, the private sector has had to purchase government information. According to a report published by the European Commission (European Commission, n.d.), PSI is crucial to the well-functioning of the internal market, free circulation of goods, services, and people.

This new data that is being referred to as "open data" and "big data" is characterized by volume, velocity, and variety (Ballad et al., 2014). Its innovative and transformational power hinge on its quality which can only be achieved through information governance. Lundqvist (2013a) was of the view that European wide markets derived from PSI have been estimated at a turnover of 30 billion Euros per year. The PSI can be defined "as any kind of information that is produced and/or collected by a public body and it is part of the institution's mandated role" (Dragos & Neamtu, 2009, p. 4). The PSI, e.g., constitutes data in geographical information systems, land registry, public weather services, and other types of information that are created by public administrations. The Directive even covers written texts, databases, audio files, and film fragments (The European Union, 2003). Access to PSI is meant to stimulate the development of information markets and to improve the quality of e-Government services. However, this data does not only offer opportunities, but also poses risks to organizations because it is gathered from different sources which can complicate the trace of its provenance. Further, it is big volume and flows at a speed which makes it difficult to be subjected to human review. It also offers an opportunity for correlation with other datasets which means that it can be used for different purposes, and even for criminal purposes which could be detrimental for organizations (Ballad et al., 2014).

The Swedish e-Government Delegation's report, e.g., emphasized the effective management of information in the development of the third generation e-Government. The third generation e-Government aims to develop a demand driven e-Government that also considers the society around it, that is, the citizens and private companies. They are looked upon as capable e-Government co-developers with the capability to use government information to develop new services and hence increase the innovation and development potential of the society at large. The management of information, therefore, ought to be coordinated to reduce the administrative burden and to make it easily accessible in order to facilitate business transactions (Finansdepartmenetet, 2009:86). Research that was carried out in two Swedish municipalities however confirmed that as e-Government development projects are undertaken to improve service delivery, information management is not usually at the center of these projects. This is paradoxical because effective processes require good quality information and the reuse of information requires that government organizations put in place long-term preservation strategies to guarantee access to their information resources for current and future users (Svärd, 2010, 2014). The pluralization of government information resources will require a holistic approach that entails managing the information continuum if information is to be repurposed. The PSI is a good example of how information created to conduct government business can be made available to other actors to develop new services.

1.3 Information infrastructure

Information underpins the functions of government. Information management is therefore of paramount importance to e-Government development, an initiative with the ultimate goal of effective service delivery and increased accountability and transparency. Authors such as Headayetullah & Pradhan (2010) contended that the amalgamation of government information resources and the interoperation of autonomous information systems are crucial to the achievement of e-Government development goals. Some of the critical factors of e-Government development include information and data management and organizational collaboration (Melin & Axelsson, 2009). Satish and Thompson (2012) examined the complementary role of governance dimensions such as; voice and accountability, political stability, government effectiveness, regulatory control, rule of law, and control of corruption on the relationship between a country's information infrastructure and its e-Government development. They posited that several studies that have examined e-Government development facilitators emphasize the need for a robust and reliable information infrastructure. Information infrastructure is defined as, "all computerized networks, applications and services that citizens can use to access, create, disseminate, and utilize digital information." However, e-Government development is not only contingent on the information infrastructure but governance is equally important (Satish & Thompson, 2012, p. 1931). Scholars such as Stamoulis, Gouscos, Georgiadis & Martakos (2001) argued that one of the core issues that must be addressed during e-Government development is the information management philosophy that underlies information communication technology (ICT) investments. An appropriate information management strategy must be in place to facilitate decision making processes. They further recommended a proactive exploitation of the public information treasure instead of the reactive response to information requests. This is what will shape a new philosophy in public information management.

If information is to be leveraged via the Internet to harness the general public's opinion in policy development processes, it needs to be securely managed and coordinated. Citizens expect some degree of homogeneity in government information and government departments need to standardize and package information in a manner that meets with the citizens' demands and expectations (Richard, 1999). e-Government development challenges therefore include lack of information management skills required if information is to be treated like a valuable resource. Information skills from different disciplines are a necessity in managing information, content, quality, format, storage, transmission, accessibility, usability, security, and preservation (Reffat, 2003). Kaurahalme, Syväjärvi, and Stenvall's (2011) research also acknowledged that information management is the missing link between e-Government policy research and e-Government as a technology applications domain.

The biggest concerns of e-Government development are not therefore only technical (Jaeger, Paul, & Thompson, 2003). Policy issues like coordination, collaboration between agency leaders and agency-oriented thinking hinder a focus on overall goals and lack of communication. Government institutions need to move away from the traditional hierarchical and silo information management models in order to promote information sharing. This will require an integration of processes and information systems to replace the inefficient and bureaucratic ones (Sarikas & Weerakkody, 2007). There is need to change business processes, organizational structures, and the management of information systems if e-Government is to be successfully implemented (Stemberger & Indihar, 2007). It will require overcoming the challenges posed by information management. Secure and effective information management requires collaboration among different competences.

Working in silos will only continue to complicate the challenges since the digital information management environment requires that information planning is done before the information is created. Organizations need to decide on which metadata is to be used in order to steer information rightly, rules that regulate access, search possibilities, and the integration of different information systems. The digital information management environment today requires a collaboration of disciplines such as: Law; Archives and Information Science; Information Security; Business Process Analysis; and Systems Science. Lawyers would facilitate the understanding of the legal requirements which apply to the management of public information, Archivists and Records Managers would deal with the evaluation of information, classification structures and methods for registration, search and reuse of information, Information Security professionals would enhance the authenticity and reliability of the information, Business Process Analysts would promote the improvement of business processes and the identification of valuable information, Systems Scientists would ensure that legal, business requirements, knowledge on IT and information security are considered when developing information systems.

1.3.1 Electronic archiving and registration

Though transparency and accountability are quite central to e-Government development, the issue of electronic archiving and registration is not discussed by e-Government scholars. It is a fact that effective information management and use cannot take place without these two functions. The open governance structure of government institutions hinges on the fact that the processes they undertake are well documented. Therefore, electronic archiving and registration is key to the delivery of quality services, the traceability of the citizens' cases, and the transparency of decision making processes. In Sweden, e.g., the Swedish e-Government Delegation charged the Swedish National Archives with the responsibility to develop these two important areas. The project was based on the premise that without effective information management regimes it would be difficult to uphold the right to access government information both for internal and external use (Riksarkivet, n.d.). The project's objectives were to develop common specifications for government agencies that would:

- facilitate the transfer of digital records between records management systems and an electronic archive;
- to test and quality assure the specifications; and
- to propose an organization that will manage them.

This is an effort to enhance information retrieval, reuse, and transfer of information held by public authorities. Sweden promotes readily access to public records and there is no demarcation between current and archival records. The rules governing public access to government records date back to the first Freedom of the Press Act of 1776 (Gränström, Lundquist, & Fredriksson, 2000). Access to public information/records can only be achieved by undertaking archiving and registration. All Swedish government administrations are required to manage their information according to the Archival Law (Bohlin, 2010). The registration of public records is a requirement by law (Gränström et al., 2000). It is an important part of the open governance structure of Swedish public administrations. It facilitates the traceability of records and hence promotes information access.

1.3.2 The development of common specifications

As the development of e-Government continues, the hierarchical structures of government institutions are being challenged. Today, it is important that institutions collaborate across boundaries, which has also led to the development of integrated services (Asproth, 2007). In the hierarchical environment, information systems were created to serve functions of a particular department. The focus today is on processes and information systems must be aligned with the processes. Since processes stretch beyond departmental boundaries, information systems must be implemented in such a way that facilitates information sharing through integration. As per the request of the Swedish E-delegation, the Swedish National Archives undertook a project in 2011 to develop what is referred to as Förvaltningsgemensamma Specifikationer—FGS literally translated as Common Specifications. A common specification is defined as "a structured description of the functional and technical requirements that meet the needs of all or part of the government administration. A specification provides guidance when developing regulations, specifications for system procurement and when writing contracts. The purpose is to create the desired functionality and interoperability within the administration and when dealing with citizens and businesses. The FGSs are seen as a prerequisite for the establishment of inter-agency information sharing and long-term information provision. They are also meant to simplify the development, procurement and deployment of unified solutions. The ultimate goal is to reduce costs and create conditions that facilitate retrieval and reuse of information in the records" (Riksarkivet, n.d. p. 2). Additionally, Swedish institutions have espoused business process management because it creates effective business processes and facilitates the identification of key information resources.

1.3.3 Business process management and information management

Good information management entails understanding the types of information that an organization creates in order to identify valuable information and what needs to be managed for long term. This requires periodic audits to identify what information exists, where it can be found, who is responsible for it and how it can be used. Business Process Management (BPM) has been embraced by organizations to improve business performance. BPM promotes the continuous improvement of work processes. The management of processes is a prerequisite for strategic planning and the coordination of businesses. BPM has its origin in industrial engineering in order to improve business processes, enhance product quality and enables the measurement of process performance (Hammer & Champy, 1995; Ljungberg & Larsson, 2008). Effective processes rely on good quality information. The identification of vital information and records in an organization is intrinsically linked to the analysis of business processes (ISO/TS 23081-1, 2004). A good example to demonstrate this is the work that the National Archives of Sweden has been involved in. In 2009, the National Archives issued a regulation requiring all government agencies to embrace process based archival descriptions by year 2009 (Riksarkivet, 2008). This has meant abandoning a 100-year archival description and classification system. It was argued that the traditional archival description system was insufficient in the current complex digital information management environment. The traditional system was hierarchical in structure and was based on physical volumes that described the types of records instead of focusing on the content (Sundberg, 2013). It is argued that business process oriented archival descriptions suit the digital environment and hence facilitate a better understanding of the context under which the information/records are created (Samuelsson, n.d.). The archival descriptions are supposed to facilitate information access and therefore of crucial importance in an era where huge chunks of information have to be made available to the general public.

1.4 Conclusion

e-Government development goals of effective service delivery, increased transparency, and accountability through the free flow of information hinge on a proper information management infrastructure. e-Government has led to an increase in the information that government institutions need to manage well, in order to ensure that it is secure, authentic, and reliable. It further requires doing away with the hierarchical structures and embracing BPM approaches that will create efficiences and promote the sharing of information among government institutions. Effective information management is quite central to e-Government development. The emerging complex environment requires collaboration among different disciplines and hence competences that will deal with the legal, informational and security issues and systems challenges. Appropriate procedures, processes, and systems are considered necessary to provide and maintain trustworthy information for long-term in order to promote long-term transparency. If information is to be used as a national resource it has to be well planned for, structured and its entire continuum has to be managed.

References

Archmann, S. & Iglesias, C.J. (2010). eGovernment – A driving force for innovation and efficiency in Public Administration. Retrieved from http://www.eipa.eu/files/repository/eipascope/20100519110452_Eipascope_2010_1eGovernment.pdf. Accessed 13.05.22.

Asproth, V. (2007). Integrated information systems—A challenge for long-term digital preservation. *Interdisciplinary Journal of Information, Knowledge, and Management, 2*, 90–98, Retrieved from <ir.inflibnet.ac.in/dxml/handle/1944/1366>.

Ballad, C., Compert, C., Jesionowski, T., Milman, I., Plants, B., Rosen, B., & Harald, S. (2014). *Information governance principles and practices for a big data landscape.* Retrieved from <https://books.google.se/books?id=-0M5AwAAQBAJ&pg=PA74&lpg=PA74&dq=The + information+landscape&source=bl&ots=OJN66Lbnum&sig=m1m6t-XAW3IaPiRbG63DLvDJ04ng&hl=sv&sa=X&ved=0ahUKEwil8Je74M7KAhUL1ywK-HSBIBhc4FBDoAQgiMAE#v=onepage&q=The%20information%20landscape&f=false>. Accessed 16.01.29.

Bearman, D. (1994). *Electronic evidence: Strategies for managing records in contemporary organizations.* Pittsburgh: Archives & Museum Informatics.

Bohlin, A. (2010). *Offentlighetsprincipen.* Mölnlycke: Elanders Sverige AB, (Åttonde Upplaga ed.).

Directorate General of Human Rights. (2004). Access to official documents guide. Retrieved from <http://www.coe.int/t/dghl/standardsetting/cddh/Publications/DocAccess_Guide_en.pdf>. Accessed 16.01.29.

Dollar, C. M. (2000). *Authentic electronic records: Strategies for long-term access.* Chicago, IL: Cohasset Associates, Inc.

Dragos, D. C., & Neamtu, B. (2009). Reusing Public Sector Information—Policy Choices and Experiences in some of the Member States with an emphasis on the Case of Romania. *European Integration Online Papers, 13*, 1–27.

Duranti, L., & Preston, R. (2008). International Research on Permanent Authentic Records in Electronic Systems (InterPARES 2), Experiential, Interactive and Dynamic Records. Padova.

European Commission. (n.d.). Public Sector Information: A key resource for Europe. Green Paper on Public Sector Information in the Information Society. Retrieved from <ftp://ftp.cordis.europa.eu/pub/econtent/docs/gp_en.pdf>. Accessed 15.07.23.

European Union. (2003). Directive 2003/98/EC of the European Parliament and of the Council on the re-use of public sector information. *Official Journal of the European Union*. Retrieved from <http://ec.europa.eu/information_society/policy/psi/docs/pdfs/directive/psi_directive_en.pdf>. Accessed 11.03.23.

Fang, Z. (2002). E-Government in digital era: Concept, practice, and development. *International Journal of the Computer, the Internet and Management*, *10*(2), 1–22.

Finansdepartmenetet. (2009:86). *Strategi för myndigheternas arbete med e-förvaltning. Betänkande av E-delegationen*. Retrieved from Stockholm <http://www.sweden.gov.se/sb/d/11456/a/133813>. Accessed 13.02.04.

Gränström, C., Lundquist, L., & Fredriksson, K. (2000). *Arkivlagen, Bakgrund och kommentarer*. Göteborg: Graphic Systems AB, (Vol. andra upplagan).

Grant, G., & Chau, D. (2006). *Developing a generic framework for e-Government in advanced topics in global information management*. Vol. 5. In G. Hunter, M., Tan, B., Felix, (Eds.). Retrieved from <https://books.google.se/books?hl=sv&lr=&id=5Vy9AQAAQBAJ&oi=fnd&pg=PA72&dq=information+management+and+e-government+development&ots=iOlNv4Luz_&sig=KnV51jmwFi_d9L1LZatVP-xpphE&redir_esc=y#v=onepage&q=information%20management%20and%20e-government%20development&f=false>. Accessed 13.01.13.

Hammer, M., & Champy, J. (1995). Re-engineering the corporation. A manifestor for business revolution. London: Nicholas Brealey Publishing.

Headayetullah, M., & Pradhan, G. K. (2010). Interoperability, trust based information sharing protocol and security: Digital Government key issues. *International Journal of Computer Science and Information Technology*, *2*(3).

ISO/TS 23081-1. (2004). Information and Documentation—Records Management Processes – Metadata for records. Part 1 Principles.

Jaeger, P. T., & Bertot, J. C. (2010). Transparency and technological change: Ensuring equal and sustained public access to government information. *Government Information Quarterly*, *27*, 31–376.

Jaeger, P. T., & Thompson, M. K. (2003). E-government around the world: Lessons, challenges, and future directions. *Government Information Quarterly*, *20*, 389–394.

Kaurahalme, O.-P., Syväjärvi, A., & Stenvall, J. (2011). From e-Government to public information management—The maturity and future of information management in local governments, 7–10 September. In *Paper presented at the European group of public administration annual conference, Bucharest*. <http://egpa-conference2011.org/documents/PSG1/Kaurahalme-Syvajarvi-Stenvall.pdf>. Accessed 12.01.09.

Layne, K., & Lee, J. (2001). Developing fully functional E-government: A four stage model. *Government Information Quarterly*, *18*, 122–136.

Ljungberg, A., & Larsson, E. (2008). *Processbaserad verksamhetsutveckling Lund*. Studentlitteratur.

Lundqvist, B. (2013a). *"Turning government data into gold": The interface between EU Competition Law and the Public Sector Information Directive—With some comments on the Compass Case. (IIC 44)*, pp. 79–95.

Melin, U., & Axelsson, K. (2009). Managing e-service development—Comparing two e-government case studies. *Transforming Government: People, Process and Policy*, *3*(3), 248–270.

Mendel, T. (2008). *Freedom of information: A comparative legal survey*. Retrieved from <http://portal.unesco.org/ci/en/files/26159/12054862803freedom_information_en.pdf/freedom_information_en.pdf>. Accessed 15.07.05.

Nordfors, L., Ericson, B., & Lindell, H. (2016). *Vinnova report, The future of e-Government. scenarios 2016*. Retrieved from <http://www.vinnova.se/upload/EPiStorePDF/vr-06-11.pdf>. Accessed 16.01.06.

Office of Public Sector Information. (2009). *The United Kingdom report on the Re-use of Public Sector Information, unlocking psi potential*. Retrieved from <http://www.opsi.gov.uk/advice/psi-regulations/uk-report-resuse-psi-2009.pdf>. Accessed 10.12.03.

Reffat, R.M. (2003). *Developing a successful e-Government*. Retrieved from <http://faculty.kfupm.edu.sa/ARCH/rabee/publications_files/03Reffat_eGov.pdf>. Accessed 13.05.06.

Richard, E. (Ed.), (1999). *Tools of governance, digital democracy, discourse and decision making in the information age*. London: Routledge.

Regeringskansliet. 2009. Public access to information and secrecy act. Retrieved from http://www.sida.se/Global/Innovations%20Against%20Poverty/Public%20info%20Act.pdf. Accessed 12.07.04.

Riksarkivet. (n.d.). *The e-Archive and e-Diarium Project, eAR*. Retrieved from <http://riksarkivet.se/Media/pdf-filer/Projekt/eARD_informationstext_eng.pdf>. Accessed 15.04.17.

Riksarkivet. (2008). *Riksarkivets författningssamling*. (ISSN 0283-2941). Retrieved from <http://riksarkivet.se/Media/pdf-filer/RAFS%202008-4.pdf>. Accessed 15.04.17.

Samuelsson, G. (n.d.). *The new information landscape. The archivist and architect—Drawing on a common map?* Retrieved from <http://www.unesco.org/new/fileadmin/MULTIMEDIA/HQ/CI/CI/pdf/mow/VC_Samuelsson_28_D_1110.pdf>. Accessed 15.04.17.

Sarikas, D. O., & Weerakkody, V. (2007). Realising integrated e-government services: A UK local government perspective. *Transforming Government: People, Process and Policy*, *1*(2), 153–173.

Satish, K., & Thompson, S. H. T. (2012). Moderating effects of governance on information infrastructure and E-Government development. *Journal of the American Society for Information Science and Technology*, *60*(10), 1929–1946.

Scholl, J. H. (2006). Electronic government: Information management capacity, organizational capabilities, and the sourcing mix. *Government Information Quarterly*, *23*, 73–96.

Stamoulis, D., Gouscos, D., Georgiadis, P., & Martakos, D. (2001). Revisiting public information management for effective e-government services. *Information Management & Computer Security*, *9/4*, 146–153.

Stemberger, M., & Indihar, J. J. (2007). Towards E-government by business process change—A methodology for public sector. *International Journal of Information Management*, *27*, 221–232.

Sundberg, H. (2013). Process based archival descriptions—Organizational and process challenges. *Business Process Management Journal*, *19*(5), 783–798.

Svärd, P. (2010). E-Government initiatives and information management challenges in two local government authorities. In *Paper presented at the proceedings of the 4th European conference on information management and evaluation*. Portugal, Universidade Nova de Lisboa.

Svärd, P. (2014). Information and records management systems and the impact of information culture on the management of public information *(Ph.D. Degree)*. Amsterdam: University of Amsterdam. Retrieved from <http://dare.uva.nl/document/2/140656>. Accessed 15.04.12.

The International Records Management Trust. (2004). The e-records readiness tool. Retrieved from <http://www.nationalarchives.gov.uk/rmcas/documentation/eRecordsReadinessTool_v2_Dec2004.pdf>. Accessed 13.11.18.

United Nations Department of Economic and Social Affairs. (2012). E-government survey 2012. E-government for the people. Retrieved from <http://unpan1.un.org/intradoc/groups/public/documents/un/unpan048065.pdf>. Accessed 13.03.20.

Worall, L. (Ed.), (2010). *Leading issues in e-government research.* Ridgeway Press in the UK.

Worthy, B. (2010). More open but not more trusted? The effect of the Freedom of Information Act 2000 on the United Kingdom Central Government. *Governance: An International Journal of Policy, Administration, and Institutions.*, *23*(4), 561–582.

Yong, S.L.J., & Cheong, Y.N.A. (2004). Promoting citizen-centered approaches to e-Government programmes—Strategies & perspectives from Asian Economies. In *Paper presented at the second APEC high-level symposium on e-Government, Acapulco, Mexico.* <www.egov-in-asia.com/egov-2/cms.../egov-paper-for-apec.pdf>. Accessed 10.03.08.

Records management

2

2.1 The current information landscape and the proliferating information acronyms

Ideas about records, information, and content management have fundamentally changed and developed as a result of increasing digitalization. Though not fully harmonized, these new ideas commonly stress and underpin the need for a proactive and holistic information management approach. The proactive approach entails planning for the management of the entire information continuum before the information is created. For private enterprises and government institutions endeavoring to meet new information demands from customers, citizens and the society at large, such an approach is a prerequisite for accomplishing their missions. The incorporation of information technology into public and private business environments requires robust information management regimes (Mnjama & Wamukoya, 2007). Technology has led to the proliferation of the records that have to be managed. Within the context of public administrations, this is demonstrated through e-Government development.

The effective management of information in organizations has grown in importance and the New Public Management theory emphasizes the role of information in the management of performance and control of the agents' actions (Harries, 2009). The variety of information that organizations have to manage continues to grow beyond the traditional types of information they are used to. Today's information landscape requires the management of social media, content being generated by nontraditional means, instant messaging, blogs, wikis, collaboration tools, and social networks (Ballad et al., 2014). The exponential growth of digital information and the challenges it poses are overpowering. This is why it is often described with negative analogies such as "the digital deluge" and "data tsunami." Understanding what the different information management constructs and acronyms have to offer in terms of solutions, is crucial to identifying a suitable system for the efficient management of information. In this chaotic environment with gigantic volumes of digital data, information that constitutes evidence of the transactions carried out in an organization has to be managed according to best practice. This is where records management as a sub-set of information management still plays a major role. There are however many other attempts aimed at managing the current information landscape and which have resulted in various information management acronyms, promising to deliver the magic bullet towards the management of different information resources. The list includes among many, the following:

Enterprise Content Management, Records Management and Information Culture Amidst e-Government Development.
DOI: http://dx.doi.org/10.1016/B978-0-08-100874-4.00002-8

2.1.1 Document management (DM)

Document management is how an organization stores, manages and tracks its electronic documents.[1] According to ISO 12651-2, a document is recorded information or object which can be treated as a unit (ISO 15489-1, 2001).

2.1.2 Information resource management (IRM)

Techniques of managing information as a shared organizational resource. Information Resource Management (IRM) includes:

- identification of information sources;
- type and value of information they provide; and
- ways of classification, valuation, processing, and storage of that information.[2]

2.1.3 Web content management (WCM)

According to the Association for Image and Information Management Web Content Management (WCM) is similar to content management in that it manages the integrity, revisions, and life cycle of information—except it specializes in content that is specifically destined for the web.

2.1.4 Information governance (IG)

Information Governance (IG) is defined as a sort of super discipline that has emerged as a result of new and tightened legislation governing businesses, external threats such as hacking and data breaches, and the recognition that multiple overlapping disciplines are needed to address today's information management challenges in an increasingly regulated and litigated business environment. IG is a subset of corporate governance, and includes key concepts from records management, content management, IT and data governance, information security, data privacy, risk management, litigation readiness, regulatory compliance, long-term digital preservation, and even business intelligence. It further includes related technology and discipline subcategories, such as document management, enterprise search, knowledge management, and business continuity/disaster recovery (Smallwood, 2014, p. 5).

2.1.5 Enterprise content management (ECM)

Enterprise Content Management (ECM) is defined as "The strategies, tools, processes, and skills an organization needs to manage all its information assets, (regardless of type) over their lifecycle" (vom Brocke, Simons, & Schenk, 2008, p. 1049). Other authors defined ECM as "the technologies used to capture,

[1] Definition from the Association for Information and Image Management (AIIM): http://www.aiim.org/What-is-Document-Management

[2] Definition is from Business dictionary available at: http://www.businessdictionary.com/definition/information-resources-management-IRM.html#ixzz40hMVeiN8

manage, store, preserve, and deliver content and documents related to organizational processes. ECM tools and strategies allow the management of an organization's unstructured information, wherever that information exists" (MacMillan & Huff, 2009, p. 4). ECM is about the management of all content in an organization.

2.1.6 Enterprise content management and records management (ECRM)

Enterprise Content Management and Records Management is defined as "the strategy, technology, and processes for managing information assets facilitated by information technology" Strong (2008, p. 1). Strong combined Enterprise Content Management and Records Management and suggested the acronym "ECRM".

Despite the proliferating acronyms, what is most important to organizations is the effective management of their information resources regardless of whether it is records, data, or content. Records, data, and content need to be of good quality if organizations are to make sound decisions and deliver good services. All organizations need high-quality information, which has to be authentic, reliable, and complete. The information/records management function involves many people in an organization. Most people have become records creators, which means that they should have a sense of ownership and accountability to the records they create. Everyone in the organization needs to understand the records management responsibilities. This would enable an understanding needed to effectively manage key business information. Therefore, today's information environment requires holitistic, proactive, and collaborative enterprise-wide information management approaches and should engage different professions such as the IT, business process managers, business process analysts, information architects, records managers, archivists, and lawyers (Eriksson, 2014).

2.2 Records management

Records management is defined as a "field of management responsible for the efficient and systematic control of the creation, receipt, maintenance, use and disposition of records, including processes for capturing, and maintaining evidence of and information about business activities and transactions in the form of records" (ISO 15489-1, 2001, p. 7). The Archives and Information Science perspective further emphasizes the context, provenance, integrity, and authenticity of the records (Yeo, 2007). A records management system constitutes people, processes and technology. Records differ from other information assets because of the inherent transactional characteristics that make them reliable and authentic (Reed, 2005). Good records management underpins good governance and is of crucial importance in a digital environment where, records can easily be tampered with and manipulated. Government records are a source of public accountability of those we vote into power to manage our common public goods. These are people we expect to manage the public trust that mandates them to make decisions on our behalf as citizens.

2.3 Records and their role in society

Records are the evidence of actions and decisions, and therefore trustworthy records are the pillars of accountability and transparency. According to ISO 15489-1 (2001, p. 7) records are "information created, received, and maintained as evidence and information by an organization or person in pursuance of legal obligations or in the transaction of business." ISO 15489-1 provides best practice guidance on how records should be managed to ensure they are authentic, reliable, complete, unaltered, and usable. It is further argued in the guidelines of the International Council on Archives that a record is "not just a collection of data, but is the consequence or product of an event and therefore linked to a business activity. A distinguishing feature of records is that their content must exist in a fixed form, that is, be a fixed representation of the business transaction" (International Council on Archives, 2008a, p. 11). In order for a document to be referred to as a record, it should have the following characteristics:

- Authenticity—The record can be proven to be what it purports to be, to have been created or sent by the person that created or sent it, and to have been created or sent at the time it is purported to have occurred.
- Reliability—The record can be trusted as a full and accurate representation of the transaction(s) to which they attest, and can be depended on in the course of subsequent transactions.
- Integrity—The record is complete and unaltered, and protected against unauthorized alteration. This characteristic is also referred to as "inviolability."
- Usability—The record can be located, retrieved, preserved, and interpreted (International Council on Archives, 2008a).

Shepherd (2006) looked at the role of records in the public sector and postulated that records are kept because they have the following values:

- They enable decisions to be made and actions taken and hence provide access to precedents and policies, and evidence of what was done or decided in the past.
- They enable organizations to guard against fraud and to protect their rights and assets.
- They support accountability and organizations are accountable in many ways, to meet legal, regulatory, and fiscal requirements, undergo audits and inspections, or provide explanations for what was done. Internally, records are used to prove or assess performance. External accountability is especially important to public sector bodies, which are responsible for their actions to government and the wider public.
- They may also be used for cultural purposes for research, to promote awareness and understanding of corporate history. The wider community also has expectations of transparency in public service, the protection of rights and the maintenance of sources for collective memory.

Therefore records attest the transactions that take place in an organization and it is their evidentiary value that makes them different from documents. A record has to be maintained in a manner that sustains its integrity, authenticity, and reliability. These characteristics are a challenge to maintain in the digital environment. Therefore, a record's structure, context, and metadata are critical to its authentication. The structure is related to how the record is recorded and includes the use of symbols, layout, format, and medium. Electronic records however have a physical and logical structure. The physical structure of an electronic record is variable and is dependent on soft and hardware. The logical structure constitutes the relationship of a record's component parts, which make it intelligible. The context of a record is vital when it comes to understanding the links it has had with its administrative and functional environment which created it. Yet metadata which is defined as data about data, covers the contextual information, content and structure and is key to the management of records for long term (International Council on Archives, 2008b).

Records are a means of power that governments use not only to exercise control over citizens, but also as a means of citizens' empowerment. They are instruments that governments can use to build trust in government institutions and hence a foundation of accountability, where their integrity and authenticity is well managed (International Records Management Trust, 2000). Freedoms of expression and access to information are cornerstones of modern democracies. Through access to government records the citizens can assess the performance of government, call for responsibility and accountability, demand compensation for injustice, and enhance their knowledge and freely evolve opinions. It is stated in the Council of Europe's report of 2009 (The Council of Europe, 2009) that access to public records is of paramount importance in a pluralistic and democratic society. The right to access public records therefore:

- provides a source of information for the public;
- helps the public to form an opinion on the state of society and on public authorities; and
- fosters the integrity, efficiency, effectiveness and accountability of public authorities, so helping affirm their legitimacy.

The report further states that all government records are in principle public and that the public can only be denied access if it is for the protection of other rights and legitimate interests. In order to fulfill these objectives, adequate, efficient and accountable records management procedures are required. Transparency, accountability, and good governance hinge on how well governments document their operations and the interactions they have with the citizens. The information that governments generate must be trustworthy and complete. Government records make up government archives and Iacovino (2010, p. 183) quoted Eastwood who referred to "archives as arsenals of democratic accountability and continuity into society and into its very corporate and social fabric." Bishop Desmond Tutu once postulated that archives contain records that are "a potent bulwark against human rights violations" (Wilson, 2012). In order to promote access, government information has to be well managed.

The trend towards greater transparency continues and many countries have adopted Freedom of Information laws. In Sweden, for example, all government institutions have the obligation to manage the information that they receive and produce to promote the right to access public records (Gränström, Lundquist, & Fredriksson, 2000). Access to public records hinges on good records management systems. It would be difficult for any government to promote the Freedom of Information legislation without a well-functioning records management system, to facilitate the capture, management, search, preservation, retrieval, and dissemination of records regardless of format. It is also important that the information that is put in the public domain is complete, authentic, and usable and therefore the provenance of the records that the public accesses matters. Poor records management regimes are likely to cause loss of corporate memory, inefficiency and an inability to meet accountability and legislative requirements (International Council on Archives, 2008a).

2.4 Provenance

The provenance of the records is central to establishing their authenticity and enables the records to be traced to their original source. Provenance refers to "the office of origin' of records, or that office, administrative entity, person, family, firm, from which records, personal papers, or manuscripts originate" (Winget, 2004, p. 1). It is crucial to understanding the history of creation, ownership and changes made to records (Factor et al., 2009). Provenance is also referred to as "respect des fonds," and the International Research on Permanent Authentic Records in Electronic Systems (InterPARES 2) defined provenance as "the relationships between records and the organizations or individuals that created, accumulated and/or maintained and used them in the conduct of personal or corporate activity" (Duranti & Preston, 2008, p. 831). The principle of provenance is crucial in the digital networked environment and has relevance to e-Government, because it points out which organizations are responsible for the management of the entire records continuum. Upward (2009) argued that it is essential for electronic records to be identified and managed in a manner that will make them accessible for as long as they are of value.

The National Electronic Commerce Coordinating Council (2004) quoted the following as the six fundamental challenges in maintaining confidence and trustworthiness in electronic records:

- Classification: Develop and adopt data classification standards to protect information from unauthorized or accidental disclosure, modification, or loss. Data classification categories may be as simple as "Open" or "Confidential," or the classification categories may be more elaborate. Classification standards should be based on applicable laws, legal, and regulatory requirements, not individual desires.
- Authenticity: Provide assurances that every record truly originates from its attributed author.
- Integrity: Detect and track unintentional or malicious record alteration.
- Nonrepudiation: Prevent authors from refuting any record that they created.
- Security Persistence: Maintain a document's security throughout its lifecycle, from first draft to archived record, per the classification assigned.
- Usability: Finally, the practices and policies to address the five preceding challenges should be easy to understand and easy to use so that everyone in an organization who creates and accesses electronic documents protects document confidentiality, authenticity, integrity, etc.

As governments engage in e-Government development they need to address any obstacles that might hinder the effective management of government records and demonstrate that they have e-readiness in place.

2.4.1 E-readiness

Duranti and Preston (2008), who were involved in the InterPARES 2 research into electronic records creation and use, stated that the context under which records creators operate today is collaborative and records creation is therefore distributed. This environment requires the maintenance of reliable and authentic records. Information systems need to be trustworthy to enhance public trust and the public bodies' accountability (Duranti & Preston, 2008). The effective management of electronic records amidst e-Government development requires e-readiness which has been defined by Lipchak and McDonald (2003, p. 1) as, "the capacity to create, manage, share, and use electronic information (and related technology) to improve governance as well as sustain international trade and innovation; improve global security and support other activities in our increasingly interconnected and interdependent world." The e-Government development environment requires an information infrastructure that should facilitate the effective capture of records as information of evidence. However, despite technological advancements, the management of records still poses challenges (Svärd, 2014).

Cunningham (2011) investigated Australian government agencies and confirmed that they are still lagging when it comes to the management of digital records. This is a surprise since Australia is at the cutting edge when it comes to the development of international standards in the records management field. Sweden is one of the leading countries in e-Government development but research that was conducted by Svärd (2014) in some of its municipalities revealed that the management of information is still a challenge and many government agencies still lack electronic archives (Riksarkivet, n.d.). Technological developments have resulted in sophisticated tools that are used by organizational employees. Where there is no information governance, public records end up in personal systems which puts the information under the control of individuals (Svärd, 2014; The National Electronic Commerce Coordinating Council, 2004).

Therefore, lack of e-readiness complicates the management of digital records as evidence and hence loss of rights. It poses the following challenges:

- lack of accountability for the management of e-records (who is responsible for protecting their integrity and authenticity?);
- complex, fragmented, and incompatible information systems and standards (e.g., computer systems and metadata standards);
- fragile, quickly changing record media, formats, and storage systems (the e-preservation challenge);
- unconnected or poorly integrated paper and electronic records and duplicated e-records (where is the complete file, the right version?);
- the lack of e-records skills (among both users and information managers); and
- limited collaboration among information professions (records managers, archivists, librarians, IT specialists, web content managers, etc.) (Lipchak & McDonald, 2003).

Lipchak and McDonald (2003) were further of the view that e-readiness requires organizational employees who are aware of the value of records, effective laws, policies to guide records management, governance, and accountability arrangements that provide organization and leadership for records management programs, the management of the records continuum, collaboration among all professions in the information management domain, training of staff and cost-effective computer systems. Their views were also supported by Mnjama and Wamukoya (2007) who carried out a literature review on ICT, records management, and e-governance, and argued that in order for a country to assess whether it is ready to manage e-records, it has to examine the legal and regulatory framework, the physical infrastructure, procedures for collecting, processing, storing and disseminating e-records, staffing and training levels, long-term preservation, and the accessibility of the records. They concluded that even though many governments have tools and procedures for managing paper records, electronic records, and digital images management is still lacking. To demonstrate the necessity of e-readiness amidst e-government development, Lowry's (2013) study that he carried out in Uganda, Kenya, and Tanzania confirmed that even though the three governments were engaging ICTs to create digital working environments, the records management systems were still very weak. The e-records infrastructure should constitute the following:

- wide awareness of the value of records by political leaders, public servants, citizens and NGOs;
- effective laws and policies to guide information management, such as, "Public Records" laws, archival legislation, access and privacy laws, policies on documenting business activities and decisions, etc.;
- governance and accountability arrangements that provide organization and leadership for records management programs, assign responsibility and encourage close collaboration among records managers, archivists, librarians, program managers, information technology specialists, etc.;
- consistent and effective standards and practices for life-cycle records management processes such as creating, organizing, classifying, storing, protecting, retrieving, retaining, destroying, and archiving electronic and paper records;
- trained staff including all civil servants and information managers who are positioned to influence and guide change;
- cost-effective computer-based systems, applications, etc. to create, manage, distribute, and use records in all forms; and
- adequate budget, space, and supplies for managing and protecting both paper and electronic records (Lipchak & McDonald, 2003).

A project entitled Accelerating Positive Change in Electronic Records Management (AC + erm) that was conducted between 2007 and 2010, confirmed that few organizations have an articulated vision for electronic records management and that the people issues were predominant, fundamental, and challenging. Records management challenges are not only technical but the people issues such as: culture, philosophical attitudes, lack of records management knowledge and skills are posing enormous challenges to the effective management of records (McLeod, Childs, & Hardiman, 2010). Organizations need to create and promote awareness among all staff members, carry out training, and implement user-friendly technologies that would motivate the staff members to leave their personal embedded practices that do not promote good records management practices. Evolving records management culture requires policy development which would assign accountability to the appropriate levels of staff (Daum, 2007).

2.5 Electronic records management systems

The development of new information technologies and organizational forms require the integration of records management. Combined, complex and automated e-services and interdepartmental cooperation will necessitate the establishment of methods and systems to guarantee compatibility and the usage of electronic records (Sundberg & Wallin, 2005). In organizations where employees manage records in an *ad-hoc* manner and use technologies not suitable for reinforcing good records management practices, there is a risk for lost productivity and increased storage and maintenance costs. Deploying the right systems to manage electronic records is crucial to the maintenance of authentic records. The functional requirements placed on Electronic Records Management Systems (ERMS) are listed in the International Council on Archives publication entitled "Principals and Functional Requirements for Records" in Electronic Office Environments. Module 2 Guidelines and Functional Requirements for ERMS that is freely available on the Internet (International Council on Archives, 2008a). ERMS should ensure the effective capture, maintenance and retrieval of records and are supposed to maintain the characteristics of a record that are: authenticity, reliability, completeness, and integrity.

2.6 Conclusion

Given the nature of the current information landscape there is need to understand what the different information management constructs and acronyms entail if the right solutions are to be deployed. Records management still has a crucial role to play amidst the different emerging information management constructs because it focuses on information of evidence, which is crucial to the protection of the rights of the citizens. A proactive and holistic approach to information and records management is central to e-Government development. This proactive approach should include long-term preservation strategies of information, to enhance long-term transparency.

As e-Government development continues governments need to invest in good records management practices. This is because the transparency of governments hinges on access to their records. Good governance, information security, and records management are intrinsically linked. Good records management regimes are a necessity in a digital networked environment and need to be espoused by all organizational employees. Organizations should involve records and archives management professionals in the legislative, planning, and operating work of information management. The quality of information will only be guaranteed by robust information management regimes. The increase in the channels through which citizens interact with government agencies requires robust information and records management systems that will capture the communication that transpires and the information and records created during the various interactions.

Further, if information is to be effectively used as a resource to boost national development, organizations need to develop a good understanding of the information management challenges at hand in order to promote a positive information culture. In theory, there are good prospects to maintain satisfactory information and records management practices. In practice, there is a problem of implementation and compliance. Research confirms that despite the importance of information as a resource in modern organizations, there are still weaknesses in its management (Anderson, 2009; Lundell & Lings, 2010; Shepherd, Stevenson, & Flinn, 2010). The burgeoning information needs to be managed in an effective way in order to comply with the rules and regulations governing public information and to achieve the objectives of e-Government development.

References

Anderson, K., Borglund, E., & Sundqvist, A. (2009). *Slutrapport. Elektronisk informations- och dokumenthantering i storajärnvägsinfrastrukturprojekt. Unpublished report.* Härnösand: Mid Sweden University.

Ballad, C., Compert, C., Jesionowski, T., Milman, I., Plants, B., Rosen, B., & Harald, S. (2014). Information governance principles and practices for a Big Data Landscape. Retrieved from <https://books.google.se/books?id=-0M5AwAAQBAJ&pg=PA74&lpg=PA74&dq=The+information + landscape&source=bl&ots=OJN66Lbnum&sig=m1m6tXAW3IaPiRbG63DLvDJ04ng&hl=sv&sa=X&ved=0ahUKEwil8Je74M7KAh-UL1ywKHSBIBhc4FBDoAQgiMAE#v=onepage&q=The%20information%20landscape&f=false>. Accessed 16.01.29.

Cunningham, A. (2011). Good digital records don't just "Happen": Embedding digital recordkeeping as an organic component of business processes and systems. *Archivaria*, *71*, 21–34.

Daum, P. (2007). Evolving the records management culture: From ad hoc to adherence. *The Information Management Journal*, 42–49.

Duranti, L., & Preston, R. (2008). International Research on Permanent Authentic Records in Electronic Systems (InterPARES 2), Experiential, Interactive and Dynamic Records, Padova.

Eriksson, J. (2014). *Öppna Myndigheten. Informaiton och ärenden i e-förvaltningen.* Lettland: Livonia Print.

Factor, M., Henis, E., Naor, D., Rabinovici-Cohen, S., Reshef, P., Ronen, S.,... Guercio, M. (2009). Authenticity and Provenance in Long-Term Digital Preservation: Modeling and Implementation in Preservation Aware Storage. Retrieved from <http://portal.acm.org/citation.cfm?id = 1525938>. Accessed 11-04-27.

Gränström, C., Lundquist, L., & Fredriksson, K. (2000). *Arkivlagen, Bakgrund och kommentarer*. Göteborg: Graphic Systems AB, (Vol. andra upplagan,).

Harries, S. (2009). Managing records, making knowledge and good governance. *Records Management Journal*, *19*(No. 1), 16–25.

Iacovino, L. (2010). Archives as arsenals of accountability. In T. Eastwood, & H. MacNeil (Eds.), In currents of *archival thinking*. Santa Barbara, CA: Libraries Unlimited.

International Council on Archives. (2008a). *Principles and functional requirements for records in electronic office environments—Module 2: Guidelines and functional requirments for electronic records management systems*. International Council on Archives.

International Council on Archives. (2008b). *Principles and functional requirements for records in electronic office environments—Module 2: Guidelines and functional requirements for electronic records management systems*. Retrieved from <www.ica.org>. Accessed 13.04.04

International Records Management Trust (2000). *Managing records as the basis for effective service delivery and public accountability in development: An introduction to core principles for staff of the World Bank and its partners*.

ISO 15489-1. (2001). *Information and documentation—Records management. Part 1 General*. Stockhom: SIS Förlag AB.

Lipchak, A., & McDonald, J. (2003). *Electronic government and electronic records: E-records readiness and capacity building*. Retrieved from <http://www.irmt.org/documents/research_reports/e_discussions/IRMT_ediss_readiness.pdf>. Accessed 16.02.19.

Lowry, J. (2013). Correlations between ICT and records policy integration and court case management system functionality. *Records Management Journal*, *23*(1), 51–60.

Lundell, B., & Lings, B. (2010). *How open are local government documents in Sweden? A case for open standards* (pp. 177–187). International Federation for Information Processing, (IFIP AICT 319).

MacMillan, A., & Huff, B. (2009). *Transforming Infoglut! A pragmatic strategy for Oracle Enterprise Content Management, manage corporate-wide content and intellectual property*. USA: The McGraw-Hill Companies Inc.

McLeod, J., Childs, S., & Hardiman, R. (2010). *The AC + erm Project. Funded by the Arts & Humanities Research Council (AHRC) Grant Number: AH/D001935/1*. Retrieved from <http://www.northumbria.ac.uk/static/5007/ceispdf/final.pdf>. Accessed 11.10.13.

Mnjama, N., & Wamukoya, J. (2007). E-government and records management: An assessment tool for e-records readiness in government. *The Electronic Library*, *25*(No. 3), 274–284.

Reed, B. (2005). Records. In S. McKemmish, M. Piggot, B. Reed, & F. Upward (Eds.), *Archives: Record keeping in society*. Wagga Wagga: Centre for Information Studies.

Riksarkivet. (n.d.). *The e-Archive and e-Diarium Project, eAR*. Retrieved from <http://riksarkivet.se/Media/pdf-filer/Projekt/eARD_informationstext_eng.pdf>. Accessed 15.04.17

Shepherd, E. (2006). Why are records in the public sector organizational assets? *Records Management Journal*, *16*(1), 6–12.

Shepherd, E., Stevenson, A., & Flinn, A. (2010). Information governance, records management, and freedom of information: A study of local government authorities in England. *Government Information Quarterly*, *27*(4), 337–345.

Smallwood, R. , F. (2014). *Information governance, concepts, strategies and best practices*. Hoboken, New Jersey: John Wiley & Sons, Inc.

Strong, K. (2008). Enterprise content and records management. *Journal of AHIMA*, *80* (No. 2), 38–42.

Sundberg, H., & Wallin, P. (2005). *Icebergs drifting apart?—Customer strategies affecting systems development and information management*. Paper presented at the IADIS International Conference e-Society Qawra, Malta. <www.iadis.net/dl/final_uploads/200505C045.pdf>. Accessed 11.10.18.

Svärd, P. (2014). Information and records management systems and the impact of information culture on the management of public information *(PhD Degree)*. University of Amsterdam, Amsterdam. Retrieved from <http://dare.uva.nl/document/2/140656>. Accessed 15.04.12.

The Council of Europe. (2009). Council of Europe Convention on Access to Official Documents. Retrieved from <http://www.conventions.coe.int/Treaty/en/Treaties/Html/205.htm>. Accessed 09.04.27.

The National Electronic Commerce Coordinating Council. (2004). Challenges *in managing records in the 21st century*. Retrieved from <https://library.osu.edu/assets/Uploads/RecordsManagement/Challenges-in-21st-e-recs-neccc.pdf>. Accessed 16.01.18.

Upward, F. (2009). Structuring the records continuum—part one: Postcustodial principles and properties. Retrieved from <http://www.infotech.monash.edu.au/research/groups/rcrg/publications/recordscontinuum-fupp1.html>. Accessed 11.12.02.

vom Brocke, J., Simons, A., & Schenk, B. (2008). *Transforming design science research into practical application: Experiences from Two ECM teaching cases*. Paper presented at the 19th Australasian Conference on Information Systems, Christchurch.

Wilson, I.E (2012). *"Peace, Order and Good Government": Archives in Society*. Archival Science, 12, pp. 235–244.

Winget, M. (2004). The archival principles of provenance and its application to image representation systems. Retrieved from <www.unc.edu/~winget/research/provenance.pdf>. Accessed 11.05.25.

Yeo, G. (2007). Concepts of record (1): Evidence, information, and persistent representations. *The American Archivist*, *70*(Fall/Winter 2007), 315–343.

Enterprise content management (ECM)

3

3.1 Enterprise content management

The increase in the amount of information that organizations need to manage has led to new information management constructs such as Enterprise content management (ECM). Smith and McKeen (2003) postulated that ECM is an emerging concept that academics, managers and vendors are trying to understand through research. The management of content is referred to as content management or ECM. ECM is an overarching term that refers to a number of different technologies used in the management of content (Iverson & Burkart, 2007). ECM is used to deal with the issue of vertical applications, island architectures, and it serves as a unified repository for all types of content (Kampffmeyer, 2004). Bantin (2008) postulated that ECM emerged around year 2000 as an application that combines the functionality of enterprise document management systems with service of content management application. This point of view is further confirmed by Kemp (2006), who stated that ECM systems are comparatively new and are believed to be advancements of Electronic Document Management Systems. Iverson and Burkart (2007) claimed that ECM began as a mechanism for staging and publishing web material.

ECM has evolved to address business needs at an enterprise level and to integrate traditionally independent content management technologies like document management, enterprise collaboration, knowledge management, email management, archiving solution, records management, and web content management, all in a unified platform. The literature review on ECM revealed that ECM is variably defined as a technology, an initiative, a framework, and skills (Glazer, Jenkins, & Schaper, 2005; Jenkins, Köhler, & Shackleton, 2006; MacMillan & Huff, 2009; Nordheim & Päivärinta, 2004; Smith & McKeen, 2003). MacMillan and Huff (2009) further argued that ECM is about the people in an organization, the context and content, and lastly about the technology.

The proliferation of unstructured information in organizations is one of the key drivers of ECM. ECM focuses on the management of content, a term used to cover a broad range of digital assets, including web content management, document management, and content management (Laplante & Guenette, 2000).

Enterprise Content Management, Records Management and Information Culture Amidst e-Government Development.
DOI: http://dx.doi.org/10.1016/B978-0-08-100874-4.00003-X

3.2 Enterprise content management definitions

ECM is variably defined and below are a couple of definitions offered by different authors:

> Grahlmann, Helms, Hilhorst, Brinkkemper, Van Amerongen, and Sander (n.d., p. 12) defined ECM as "the strategies, processes, methods, systems, and technologies that are necessary for capturing, creating, managing, using, publishing, storing, preserving, and disposing content within and between organizations. ECM is therefore designed to help organizations to manage their information resources effectively and in a manner that gives them a competitive edge (Glazer et al., 2005; MacMillan & Huff, 2009; vom Brocke, Derungs, et al., 2008). MacMillan & Huff contended that ECM is about creating the culture of sharing information. Shegda and Gilbert (2009) posited that ECM consists of the vision and framework to integrate a broad range of content management technologies and content formats in the entire organization.
>
> Gilbert, Shegda, Chin, Tay, and Koehler-Kruener (2014, p. 1) defined ECM both as "a strategic framework and a technical architecture that supports all types of content (and format) throughout the content life cycle."
>
> Munkvold, Päivärinta, Hodne, and Stangeland (2006, p. 69) presented it as an "integrated enterprise-wide management of the life cycles of all forms of recorded information content and their metadata, organized according to corporate taxonomies, and supported by appropriate technological and administrative infrastructures."
>
> Nordheim and Päivärinta (2004) defined ECM as "an integrated approach to managing all of an organization's information strategies, processes, skills, and tools" (Nordheim & Päivärinta, 2004, p. 1)."
>
> Jenkins, Köhler and Shackleton defined ECM as "a philosophical approach and the underlying technologies used to help businesses transform content into competitive advantage" (Jenkins et al., 2006, p. 63).
>
> Vom Brocke, Seidel, and Simons defined ECM as "The strategies, tools, processes, and skills an organization needs to manage all its information assets (regardless of type) over their lifecycle" (vom Brocke, Simons, & Schenk, 2008, p. 1049).
>
> MacMillan and Huff defined it as "the technologies used to capture, manage, store, preserve, and deliver content and documents related to organizational processes. ECM tools and strategies allow the management of an organization's unstructured information, wherever that information exists" (MacMillan & Huff, 2009, p. 4). This definition was adopted in 2006 by the Association for Information and Image Management, and it is the definition that is used by most ECM vendors.
>
> de Carvalho (2007, pp. 173–183) "ECM integrates the management of structured, semi-structured, and unstructured information, and related software and metadata in solutions for content production, publication, utilization, and storage in organizations, emphasizing the coexistence of technical and social aspects within the content management."

The above definitions demonstrate that there is no single adopted definition of ECM. Based on the definitions we can conclude that the concept is not only about a technical system or systems, but it also entails the development of policies, strategies, and skills to facilitate enterprise wide information management. ECM has also become a blanket term to cover information technologies used to manage unstructured content. Kemp (2006) posited that ECM is an aspiration to link an enterprise's intellectual assets (content) and document systems to business processes in order to enhance effective utilizations. There are however different ECM strategies and different ways of applying them. An organization can decide to implement ECM department by department or across the entire organization (MacMillan & Huff, 2009). Smith and McKeen wrote that an effective ECM strategy should address the following lifecycle stages:

- Capture—all activities associated with collecting content;
- Organize—indexing, classifying, and linking content and databases together to provide access within and across business units and functions;
- Process—sifting and analyzing content in ways that inform decision-making; and
- Maintain—ensuring that content is kept up-to-date (Smith & McKeen, 2003).

ECM can help organizations to control their content and hence boost productivity, promote collaboration, meet with compliance initiatives, promote better content-centric processes which make information easily accessible and easy to share (Gilbert et al., 2014).

ECM may be a single system dealing with different types of content and records requirements or a collection of repositories and applications. ECM proponents claim to have integrated records management into the ECM strategy in order to enable organizations to meet with compliance issues (MacMillan & Huff, 2009). It constitutes a platform or a set of applications mentioned below that interoperate but that can be sold and used separately:

- *Document management*, for check-in/check-out, version control, security, and library services for business documents.
- *Web content management* (WCM, for controlling a website's content through the use of specific management tools based on a core repository).
- *Records management*, for long-term archiving, automation of retention and compliance policies, and ensuring legal, regulatory, and industry compliance.
- *Image-processing applications*, for capturing, transforming, and managing images of paper documents.
- *Social content*, for document sharing and collaboration support for project teams and knowledge management use cases. Blogs, wikis, and support for other online interactions are evaluated.
- *Content workflow*, for supporting business processes, routing content, assigning work tasks and states, and creating audit trails. The minimum requirement is simple document review and approval workflow.
- *Extended components*, which can include one or more of the following: mobile applications, digital asset management, search, analytics and packaged integration capabilities (for portals, ERP and CRM, for example) (Gilbert et al., 2014).

3.3 ECM development driving factors

Butler Group (2003), a leading provider of information technology research, analysis, and advice, identified the reasons below as answers to why developments around content management have arisen:

- Increased volume of content which organizations must manage;
- Increased regulations and standards that require organizations to manage their content better;

- The need to track content to cater for organizational needs;
- The global nature of e-business;
- Mobile and remote working that requires that employees access information regardless of where they are and by what medium;
- The fact that organizations now recognize the monetary implications of reusing and repurposing content;
- The value of content is more tangible and some organizations have started charging for it; and
- Protection of the environment by less use of paper and scarce resources.

3.4 Structured, weakly structured, and unstructured content

Tyrväinen, Päivärinta, Salminen, and Livari (2006) referred to content as assets such as documents, websites, intranets, and extranets. Kampffmeyer (2004) went further and divided content into three categories:

- Structured content—Data delivered in a standardized layout from database-supported systems (e.g., formatted data sets from a database).
- Weakly structured content—Information and documents that may include layout and metadata, but that are not standardized (e.g., word processing files).
- Unstructured content—Any kind of information objects whose contents cannot be directly referenced and which lacks separation of content, layout, and metadata (e.g., images, GIFs, video, language, and faxes).

3.5 The ECM salient factors

The literature review that the author undertook during her PhD research (Svärd, 2014) identified the following factors to be of key importance to the effective management of content:

- Business process management;
- Collaboration;
- Change management;
- Repurposing of information;
- Knowledge management;
- System integration;
- Enterprise architecture; and
- Lifecycle management of information (Glazer et al., 2005; Jenkins et al., 2006; MacMillan & Huff, 2009).

3.5.1 *Enterprise architecture*

The successful deployment of information systems ought to be based on enterprise architecture. This is because enterprise architecture enables good decision-making

Figure 3.1 The ECM Model.
See Svärd, 2011, The Interface Between Enterprise Content Management and Records Management in Changing Organizations for reference purposes.

processes regarding information systems and how they fit the existing IT environment (Johnson & Ekstedt, 2007). The enterprise architecture models include applications, business processes, information, and the organization's IT infrastructure. Enterprise architecture has become more important to organizations as it helps them to understand the impact of technology investments on overall operations as well as assisting them with legislative compliance. It also provides the essential framework for the communication, interpretation, and implementation of corporate objectives through a well-aligned IT environment (Butler Group, 2004). Fig. 3.1 derived from a literature study on ECM mentioned above.

3.5.2 Business process management

Another prescribed factor which can strongly influence the effectiveness of ECM is business process management. The analysis of business processes enables the identification of critical business information and helps organizations to improve business operations in their entirety focusing on the input, output, the customer, and the value of the output (Hammer & Champy, 1995).

3.5.3 Change management

Change is inevitable in today's business world and once instituted, it is important that the reasons for change are effectively communicated to the personnel (Rockley, Kostur, & Manning, 2003). In order to achieve change, flexibility and responsiveness are key but this in turn requires organizational change capabilities, strong leadership, change in organizational culture and values, and a focus on customer service (Sundberg, 2006). McGreevy (2003) points out that difficulties in managing organizations through a transition should not to be underestimated. Individuals can react to changes in many ways and while some are positive, others are negative. The line managers have a crucial role to play by providing relevant explanations and information and involving those affected. This is critical to the successful implementation of change. Research on project and information systems implementation shows that top management support is a critical factor if a project is to succeed (McGreevy, 2003; Sundberg, 2006; Young & Jordan, 2008).

3.5.4 Collaboration

Collaboration is central to ECM and enables employees to dynamically work toward a common goal while capturing, storing, and archiving the content they produce. It is about openness and knowledge sharing. According to Hockman, collaboration further involves:

- Awareness of documents that are shared between departments;
- Communicating internal knowledge and experience;
- Coming up with common search terminology that will be meaningful to different departments as indexing terms;
- A shared vision for process improvement; and
- Input from every department to encourage buy-in (Hockman, 2009).

3.5.5 Knowledge management

Knowledge management is of increasing importance in modern organizations, and there are links between ECM and knowledge management. ECM implementation within organizations is underpinned by the idea and practice of information sharing. This enhances knowledge capture and knowledge transfer. While in the past knowledge has been retained in the heads of the employees, it is hoped that ECM will help organizations to retain it within the organization (Butler Group, 2004; MacMillan & Huff, 2009). Knowledge management is defined by Alavi and Leidner (2001, p. 113) as "referring to identifying and leveraging the collective knowledge in an organization to help an organization to compete." They further argue that it promotes innovativeness and responsiveness.

3.5.6 System integration

System integration allows systems to "talk" to each other and eliminates information silos (Rockley et al., 2003). The management of information systems is crucial to business operations and access to accurate and timely information hinges on how well aligned systems are with business operations. The real value from information systems, according to Themistocleous, Irani, Kuljis, and Love (2004), is from the integration of disparate applications so that they can support processes across the whole value chain.

3.5.7 The life cycle information management

The life cycle of information has to be managed and this encompasses creation, management, review, distribution, storage, and eventual disposition of information and records (MacMillan & Huff, 2009).

Conclusion

ECM is considered to be a relatively new concept and field. The literature that discusses it from a scientific point of view is only emerging. A few of the identified articles are based on formal research. The majority of the papers identified were either written by practitioners within the information technology industry or scientists in the Information Systems discipline. The ECM approach promotes knowledge management, change management, collaboration, business process management, system integration, enterprise architecture, and the life cycle management of information. Based on the literature review, one could argue ECM's potential lies in promoting the above-mentioned aspects of an enterprise-wide information management approach. It further focuses on all content in an organization whereas records management has focused on the management of authentic records. During the literature review exercise, the researcher identified two articles discussing ECM and written by scholars from the Archives and Information Science field. There is not much discourse going on between archivists/records managers and the ECM proponents. This demonstrates the need for Archives and Information Science scholars to engage in the ECM discourse. This would maintain the role that records management plays in organizations and society at large, but would also uphold the records management principles. It further demonstrates the need for more formal research in the area.

References

Alavi, M., & Leidner, D. E. (2001). Review: Knowledge management and knowledge management systems: Concepetual foundations and research issues. *MIS Quarterly*, *25*(1), 107–136.

Bantin, P. C. (2008). *Understanding data and information systems for recordkeeping*. London: Facet Publishing.

Butler Group. (2003). Enterprise content management, building a scalable and effective content infrastructure, technology evaluation and comparison report. Retrieved from

<http://www.butlergroup.com/research/reporthomepages/enterprise%20content%20management/ecm_report_management_summary.pdf> Accessed 23.05.09.

Butler Group. (2004). *Enterprise architecture. An end-to-end approach for re-aligning it with business aims*. Retrieved from <https://books.google.co.za/books/about/Enterprise_Architecture.html?id = qkzSAAAACAAJ&redir_esc = y> Accessed 23.06.09.

de Carvalho, R. Atem. (2007). An enterprise content management solution based on open source. In L. Xu, A. Tjoa, S. Chaudhry (Eds.), *IFIP, International federation for information processing, Vol. 254, Research and practical issues of enterprise information systems, Vol. 1* (pp. 173–183).

Gilbert, M. R., Shegda, K. M., Chin, K., Tay, G. & Koehler-Kruener, H. (2014). Magic quadrant for enterprise content management. Retrieved from <http://www.gartner.com/technology/reprints.do?id = 1-229MHAP&ct = 140925&st = sg> Accessed 8.01.16.

Glazer, D., Jenkins, T., & Schaper, H. (2005). *Turning content into competitive advantage, enterprise content management technology, what you need to know*. Ontario: Open Text Corporation.

Grahlmann, R. K., Helms, R., Hilhorst, C., Brinkkemper, S., & Van Amerongen, S. (n.d.). Reviewing enterprise content management: A functional framework. Retrieved from <http://remhelms.files.wordpress.com/2012/09/reviewing-enterprise-content-management-a-functional-framework-final1.pdf> Accessed 22.05.13.

Hammer, M., & Champy, J. (1995). *Re-engineering the corporation. A manifestor for business revolution*. London: Nicholas Brealey Publishing.

Hockman, H. (2009). Change management: Ensuring ECM success by preparing end-users for automation, optical image technology. Retrieved from <http://www.docfinity.com/reference/change-management-ensuring-ECM-success.htm> Accessed 2.03.10.

Iverson, J., & Burkart, P. (2007). Managing electronic documents and work flows enterprise content management at work in nonprofit organizations. *Nonprofit Management & Leadership*, *17*(4), 403–419.

Jenkins, T., Köhler, W., & Shackleton, J. (2006). *Turning content into competitive advantage, enterprise content management methods, what you need to now*. Ontario: Open Text Corporation.

Johnson, P., & Ekstedt, M. (2007). *Enterprise architecture, models and analyses for information systems decision making*. Pozkal: Studentlitteratur.

Kampffmeyer, U. (2004). Trends in record, document and enterprise content management, White paper. Retrieved from <http://www.project-consult.net/Files/ECM_Handout_english_SER.pdf> Accessed 6.11.11.

Kemp, J. (2006). A critical analysis into the use of enterprise content management systems in the IT industry. A report based on a dissertation. Retrieved from <http://www.aiimhost.com/whitepapers/JamesKemp_ECMReport.pdf> Accessed 20.12.12.

Laplante, M., & Guenette, R. D. (2000). The Gilbane Report. *What is Content? 8*(8), 1–24. Retrieved from <http://gilbane.com/artpdf/GR8.8.pdf> Accessed 20.01.12.

MacMillan, A., & Huff, B. (2009). *Transforming infoglut! A pragmatic strategy for oracle enterprise content management, manage corporate-wide content and intellectural property*. United States of America: The McGraw-Hill Companies Inc.

McGreevy, M. (2003). Managing the transition. *Industrial and Commercial Training*, *35*(6), 241–246.

Munkvold, B. E., Paivarinta, T., Hodne, A. K., & Stangeland, E. (2006). Contemporary issues of enterprise content management, the case of statoil. *Scandinavian Journal of Information Systems*, *18*(2), 69–100.

Nordheim, S., & Päivärinta, T. (2004). *Customization of enterprise content management systems: An exploratory case study*. Paper presented at the proceedings of the 37th Hawaii international conference on system sciences. Retrieved from <http://ieeexplore.ieee.org/xpl/mostRecentIssue.jsp?sortType%3Dasc_p_Sequence%26filter%3DAND%28p_IS_Number%3A28293%29&refinements=4280241177&pageNumber=1&resultAction=REFINE> Accessed 12.02.10.

Rockley, A., Kostur, P., & Manning, S. (2003). *Managing enterprise content, a unified content strategy*. New Riders.

Shegda, K. M. & Gilbert, M. R. (2009). Key issues for enterprise content management initiatives. Retrieved from <http://www.gartner.com/it/content/787300/787313/key_issues_for_enterprise_cm.pdf> Accessed 1.06.12.

Smith, A. Heather, & McKeen, D. J. (2003). Developments in practice VIII: Enterprise content management. *Communications of the Association for Information Systems*, *II*(33), 647–659.

Sundberg, H. (2006). *Problems in public e-services development. PhD Thesis (No. 11)*. Sundsvall: Mid Sweden University.

Svärd, P. (2014). *Information and records management systems and the impact of information culture on the management of public information. PhD Thesis*. Amsterdam: University of Amsterdam. Retrieved from <http://dare.uva.nl/document/2/140656> Accessed 4.03.15.

Themistocleous, M., Irani, Zahir, Kuljis, Jasna, Love, Peter E. D.,. (2004). *Extending the information system lifecycle through enterprise application integration: A case study experience*. Paper presented at the proceedings of the 37th Hawaii international conference on system sciences. Retrieved from <https://www.google.se/search?q =). + Extending + the + Information + System + Lifecycle + through + Enterprise + Application- + Integration%3A + A + Case + Study + Experience. + Proceedings + of + the + 37th + Hawaii+International+Conference+on+System+Sciences.&aq= f&oq =).+Extending + the + Information + System + Lifecycle + through + Enterprise + Application + Integration %3A+A+Case+Study+Experience.+Proceedings+of+the+37th+Hawaii+International + Conference+ on + System + Sciences.&aqs = chrome.0.57.1082j0&sourceid = chrome&ie = UTF-8> Accessed 11.09.11.

Tyrväinen, P., Päivärinta, T., Salminen, A., & Livari, J. (2006). Characterizing the evolving research on enterprise content management. *European Journal of Information Systems*, *15*, 627–634.

vom Brocke, J., Derungs, R., Ivoclar, V., Herbst, A., Novotny, S. & Simons, A. (2008). The drivers behind enterprise content management: A process-oriented perspective. Retrieved from <http://is2.lse.ac.uk/asp/aspecis/20110037.pdf> Accessed 6.10.11.

vom Brocke, J., Simons, A. & Schenk, B. (2008). *Transforming design science research into practical application: Experiences from two ECM teaching cases*. Paper presented at the 19th Australasian conference on information systems, Christchurch. Retrieved from <http://aisel.aisnet.org/cgi/viewcontent.cgi?article = 1092&context = acis2008> Accessed 12.03.11.

Young, R., & Jordan, E. (2008). Top management support: Mantra or necessity? *International Journal of Project Management*, *26*(7), 713–725.

Two principles governing the management of records

4

4.1 The life-cycle model

There are two well-recognized principles to the theory and practice of records management, namely Life-Cycle and the Records Continuum Model (RCM). The Life-Cycle Model emanates from North America and was invented and developed by the National Archives of the United States in the 1930s as a response to the exponentially growing amounts of records it had to deal with. It is also regarded as a theory that guides records management programs. At its stage of development, it covered the phases of creation, maintenance, use, and disposition (Yusof & Chell, 2000). Karabinos (2015), however, argued that the Life-Cycle Model was developed by Theodore Schellenberg and Margaret Cross Norton, who believed that archivists should be proactively involved in the decision-making process that separated records to be preserved from those that were to be destroyed. This was a response to the agencies' lack of capacity to appraise and to select records that were to be preserved. The Life-Cycle Model is further referred to as a linear model since records move in one direction, where they are either destroyed or preserved. It applies the analogy of living organisms and presumes that records are born, live, and die. This is achieved through the phases of current, semicurrent, and noncurrent where records should either be retained or disposed of (Bantin, 2008). Records are, therefore, created, used, and disposed of through destruction or preserved in the archives if they are of enduring value. Karabinos (2015, p. 24) offers the following definition of the life-cycle model:

> *The life cycle model breaks a record down into three distinct stages that distinguish records from archives. The first stage is the active stage, when records are created and actively used by the creating agency. In the second stage, the dormant stage, records are no longer of current use. The third stage is when records become archives, being stored and preserved for future use. Prior to the archival stage is the selection and appraisal process, where records are discarded or 'advanced' to the archival stage.*

Atherton (1985) contended that the Life-Cycle Model was based on the premise that a life of a record can be divided into eight stages as follows:

- creation or receipt of information in the form of records;
- classification of the records or their information in some logical system;
- maintenance and use of the records, and
- their disposition through destruction or transfer to an archive;

Enterprise Content Management, Records Management and Information Culture Amidst e-Government Development.
DOI: http://dx.doi.org/10.1016/B978-0-08-100874-4.00004-1

- selection/acquisition of the records by an archive;
- description of the records in inventories, finding aids, and the like;
- preservation of the records or, perhaps, the information in the records; and
- reference and use of the information by researchers and scholars.

Atherton (1985) was of the view that though the Life-Cycle Model has been useful in promoting a systematic way of managing paper records, it failed to acknowledge the symbiotic relationship between records and archives management. It demarcated records management from archives management hence separating the two professions that should work together to enhance an effective management of public records. In Sweden, e.g., where the profession of records manager does not exist, registrars are the ones that deal with the active management of records. Svärd's (2011b, 2014) research experience in two Swedish municipalities proved that registrars who act as "records managers" (since they deal with the active management of records) did not know much about archives management and, therefore, referred her to the archivist. Even though the archivist was actively involved in the formulation of records management strategies, such as the development of document plans, he or she was at the end of the records management life-cycle in both the investigated cases. Since the model differentiates between records managers and archivists, it has promoted a view where records managers manage records as an administrative tool while the archivists manage records for cultural and social purposes. This approach has consigned archivists to a marginal role in contemporary organizations (Brothman, 2001).

Brothman (2001) discussed the Life-Cycle and RCM in relation to the long-term use of information and argued that the Life-Cycle Model is linear and unidirectional and, therefore, loses its conceptual coherence when records reach the archival stage. He, therefore, posited that it "represents a time-ordering regime that entrenches, especially among those who control organizational resources, the business obsolescence and secondary status of aged – historical – information" (Brothman, 2001, p. 54). He believed that the Life-Cycle Model has only offered modern organizations the advantage of conceptual simplicity. This is because it has assumed simple administrations and workflow management compared to, e.g., today's reality where e-Government development has led to the development of integrated services. This has hence created more complex workflows, which involve several government institutions. Yusof and Chell (2000, p. 135) contended that the model has been rendered insufficient in the digital environment because:

> *Documents in a distributed electronic environment are dynamic and recursive in nature and may exist in more than one stage of the life cycle simultaneously. They may not follow a serial path from creation to disposal but may be reappraised at the disposition time and reappear in an earlier stage.*

The Life-Cycle Model is, therefore, regarded as more suitable to a paper-based records management system, which handles physical objects. It has facilitated the destruction of records of ephemeral value and freed office space that would have been clogged and also made retrieval of government records possible. It has, however, become insufficient in the digital environment because of the intangible nature of the digital records generated in the information management systems (Yusof & Chell, 2000). Where the Life-Cycle Model is still being used, it is equally important that it is applied during the early phases of the records life-cycle. Today's records management environment constitutes a hybrid system of paper and digital records which still renders both models important, even though the more digital organizations become the more they should employ the RCM if they are to effectively manage and use their information resources.

4.2 The Records Continuum Model

The RCM was developed by Australian theoreticians such as Peter Scott, Jay Atherton, and Frank Upward (Karabinos, 2015). The model was first clarified by Jay Atherton during a conference of the Association of the Canadian Archivists, which took place in 1985 and where he discussed the weaknesses of the Life-Cycle Model. Atherton wanted the Life-Cycle Model to be replaced by a continuum which would constituted four phases and that is:

- creation or receipt;
- classification;
- establishment of retention/disposal schedules and their subsequent implementation; and
- maintenance and use (in the creating office, inactive storage, or archives).

He regarded all the four stages as interrelated and that they required a close collaboration between the records managers and archivists (Flynn, 2001). Karabinos (2015) thus postulated that the records continuum theory developed from the work of various Australian archivists. The visual model was developed in 1990 by Frank Upward in collaboration with his colleagues: Sue McKemmish and Livia Iacovino. Reed (2005a) has also demonstrated the use of the model. The model provides a framework for the continuum of records management responsibilities (McKemmish, 1997). Upward (2000) postulated that in Australia the model is being used as a metaphor, to facilitate an understanding of records management in recordkeeping environments built around electronic communications. The model challenges the traditional view that separates archives and records as distinct entities (McKemmish, 2001). It is, therefore, defined as:

> *The whole extent of a record's existence. It refers to a consistent and coherent regime of management processes from the time of the creation of records (and before creation, in the design of recordkeeping systems), through to the preservation and use of records as archives (Yusof and Chell 2000, p. 135).*

Through its consistent and coherent management regime, the model covers the design of recordkeeping systems. This allows for the control of the precreation phase of the records, where the life-cycle begins with creation (Flynn, 2001). It considers records to always be in the process of "becoming," that is, being used in different contexts (McKemmish, 1997; Reed, 2005a). The RCM is therefore seen as a more progressive model that facilitates a proactive and holistic approach to the management of digital information. It is an approach that suits the current developments in e-Government, which are about pluralizing government information, and records for use in other contexts. A good example here is the European Union Public Sector Information Directive that the author briefly discusses in Chapter 1, e-Government development and its impact on information management, on the reuse of public information for innovative purposes (Svärd, 2014). Upward (2009) argued that the RCM is a time/space model. He contended that records continue to play different roles in a life/space model. He warned against the fracture along the lines of paper and electronic media, if recordkeeping is to be of relevance and contemporaneous to today's society. Hence, the model encourages both records managers and the archivists to meet at the critical points along the continuum (Myburgh, 2005). The model facilitates an understanding of the need to:

- develop interconnected methods for document creation;
- establish and maintain routines within which documents are captured as records; and
- control the distancing processes involved in organizing documents and records as an archive and/or as the archives.

Brothman (2001) posited the RCM has features that better could facilitate the development of a model of memory, that bolsters the pursuit of archival objectives. He was of the view that certain elements of the RCM were more compatible with the idea of social and organizational memory than the life cycle. This is because the business usefulness of archival records challenges the life-cycle representation of records. Brothman further contended that the RCM was more successful in promoting the idea of the records' indefinite business usefulness. Therefore, the RCM interpretation of the cycle leaves room for unending circular and recursive processes, which suit the contemporaneous use of records, and justifies their long-term preservation for smart organizations.

The RCM constitutes four dimensions, which are: create, capture, organize, and pluralize (Flynn, 2001, Reed, 2005a):

Dimension 1—Create: represents the locus where all business actions take place. In this dimension, documents exist in versions and can be moved beyond this locus. This dimension involves creator/creators; the transaction in which the creator/creators take part, of which a document is a result; and the document itself (with or without archival characteristics).

Dimension 2—Capture: is when a document is communicated or connected through relationships with other documents, with sequences of action. The records are in this dimension captured as evidence of transactions and can be distributed, accessed, and understood by others involved in the business transactions. This dimension involves the work unit with which the actor is associated; the activity in the context of which transactions take place; the created document together with information about its context (its provenance, or its relationships to other documents) as a record; and the evidence that results.

Dimension 3—Organize: represents an aggregation of records above individual instances of sequences of actions. Here the records are invested with explicit elements needed to ensure that they are available over time that exceeds the immediate environments of action and they join multiple other records deriving from multiple sequences of action undertaken for multiple purposes. This is the archive or fond that forms a corporate or personal memory. It is in this dimension that the organization is linked to its functions and the activities, which constitute those functions, to the archive, and to its own corporate memory.

Dimension 4—Pluralize: this dimension represents the broader social environment in which records operate. The legal and regulatory environment, which translates social requirements, different for every society, and at every period, for records management. This dimension further represents the capacity of a record/records to exist beyond the boundaries of a single creating entity.

Reed (2005b) posited that the RCM can be used for the purpose of multiple readings and that it has the capacity to support different interpretations. The model is culturally oriented and hence, open for interpretations to suit the cultural context in which the records are generated and used (Chachage & Ngulube, 2006). Dimension 4 represents the placement of records and archives in society. The (plural) archives (the records of a number of organizations) are set in the context of collective (or societal) memory (Fig. 4.1).

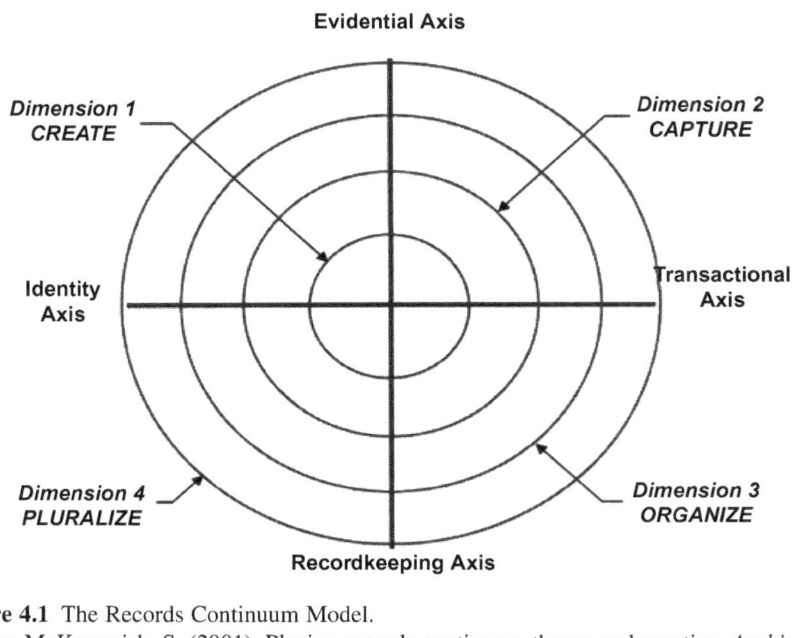

Figure 4.1 The Records Continuum Model.
Source: McKemmish, S. (2001). Placing records continuum theory and practice. *Archival Science*, *1*(4), 350.

4.3 The use of the models in practice

In theory there are best-practice models, such as the RCM that could help records managers and archivists to effectively implement and promote good information planning in organizations. Models should help people to see and understand things, but their acceptance as Upward (2000) posits depends on how much contact they make with the practical consciousness of those who are supposed to use them. Karabinos (2015) posits that the universal applicability of the RCM is not yet established but the author believes this will only be achieved if it is put to use by more people. The RCM can be used to facilitate an understanding of the emerging complex information/records management environment. This environment has become complex because of the new requirements that are placed upon government institutions. For example, European government institutions are required to free their information flows in form of data sets and this is clearly an addition to the records they have traditionally made accessible to the public. This requires robust information/records management regimes and the RCM would more effectively prepare these institutions, to package their information for pluralization compared to the Life-Cycle Model.

In an article entitled, "Reading the Records Continuum: Interpretations and Explorations" Reed (2005a) demonstrated the capacity of the RCM to support different interpretations and contexts. She argued that the model should be used as a vibrant and dynamic tool by archivists to articulate recordkeeping methodologies in different contexts. The reality, however, is different because though the RCM is quite prominent among Archives and Information Management Scientists, it is has not yet been fully embraced by practitioners and others outside the discipline. For example, Enterprise Content Management (ECM) proponents, use the Life-Cycle Model in a digital environment to manage all content and yet the RCM would have been more practical and suitable (Glazer, Jenkins, & Schaper, 2005; MacMillan & Huff, 2009). The author's supervisory work at her university in Sweden also confirms that students focusing on the model have so far not been successful in identifying organizations that use the RCM. If the challenges of managing digital information are to be effectively dealt with, information managers and information systems developers need to understand the implications of both information/records management approaches.

Karabinos (2015) posited that the proponents of the RCM see it as a replacement of the Life-Cycle Model. He however confirmed that it is the Life-Cycle Model that still dominates the management of records in many parts of the world despite the fact that the RCM was developed in 1990. In 2001, Flynn argued that records managers and archivists in the United Kingdom paid very little attention to the use of the RCM use. Svärd's (2014) research experience in two Swedish municipalities and a Belgian municipality further confirmed Karabinos' argument. Svärd (2014) drew a conclusion that none of the investigated municipalities named their information management strategies according to the two models but that it was her *a priori* knowledge of the two models that enabled her to judge the municipalities' records management strategies as life-cycle oriented. The three municipalities still lacked electronic archival repositories, which inclined them to organize their information resources as if they are still operating in a paper-based environment. The archivists in the three municipalities were quite progressive in their thinking but they were organizationally placed last at the chain of the Life-Cycle Model. Hence, information planning and management strategies would be developed without any long-term information and records management perspectives (Svärd, 2011a, 2014).

The RCM can be used as an instrument of analysis, that can facilitate an understanding of the information and records management activities that take place at each dimension along the continuum (Svärd, 2011b, 2014). This would further enable records managers and activists to address the negative attitudes that organizational employees have towards the management of public records. The RCM is about managing the entire records' continuum, which means planning for the records prior to their creation. The activities that take place under each dimension involve most people in an organization. Therefore, the effective capture of records hinges on the fact that everybody understands and appreciates the strategies put in place to facilitate the management of information and records. The negative attitudes affect the activities that take place at each of the RCM's dimensions and hence a continuum of attitudes that either promote good or bad records management.

4.4 Conclusion

In theory, there are good prospects to maintain satisfactory information and records management practices. In practice, though the RCM is considered to be the most progressive model that suits the current digital records management environment, it is the Life-Cycle Model that is mostly being espoused by organizations (Flynn, 2001; Karabinos, 2015; Svärd, 2014). The low diffusion of the RCM could be attributed to the fact that despite the early digitization of organizational processes, most organizations to date do not have electronic archives. This has maintained them in a paper-based environment, where digital information has had to be printed on paper for its effective management and to ensure its long-term preservation. This has been the practice for most organizations. The Life-Cycle Model also seems to be understood differently by the ECM systems vendors since it is the model they espouse in their ECM information management solution (MacMillan & Huff, 2009).

The burgeoning information requires effective records management regimes and close collaboration between records managers and archivists. The RCM offers archivists a chance to strategically participate in information and records management planning before the records are conceived. This also includes participating in the information systems procurement processes. Today's information environment requires collaboration among different professions in an organization. The model is not as abstract as demonstrated in the arguments that the author has heard during her teaching activities at universities and in conversation with some of the archivists she has met. The e-Government development which has led to further opening up of government information (pluralization) is a good case to demonstrate the usefulness of the RCM thinking. Information has become a useful resource that we can no longer only preserve for posterity. Progressive governments are encouraging their institutions to set government information free so that it can be used innovatively by all interested stakeholders. For governments that have invested in information management infrastructures, the citizens with the right skills and technology will benefit from this development. However, in countries with underdeveloped information infrastructures, the continued use of the Life-Cycle Model by government institutions will lead to the loss of the information that is maintained in the information systems, if investments are not made in the development of electronic archives that will facilitate the innovative re-use of government information.

References

Atherton, J. (1985). From life cycle to continuum. Some thoughts on the records management—Archives relationship. *Archivaria*, *21*, 43—51.

Bantin, P. C. (2008). *Understanding data and information systems for recordkeeping*. London: Facet Publishing.

Brothman, B. (2001). The past that archives keep: Memory, history, and the preservation of archival records. *Archivaria*, *51*, 49—80.

Chachage, B., & Ngulube, P. (2006). Management of business records in Tanzania: An exploratory case study of selected companies. *South African Journal of Information Management*, *8*(3), 1—18.

Flynn, S. J. A. (2001). The Records Continuum Model in context and its implications for archival practice. *Journal of the Society of Archivists*, *22*(1), 79—93.

Glazer, D., Jenkins, T., & Schaper, H. (2005). *Turning content into competitive advantage, enterprise content management technology, what you need to know*. Ontario: Open Text Corporation.

Karabinos, M.J. (2015). *The shadow continuum: Testing the records continuum model through the Djogdja Documenten and the migrated archives* (Ph.D. thesis). University of Leiden. Retrieved from <https://openaccess.leidenuniv.nl/bitstream/handle/1887/33293/thesis_karabinos2.pdf?sequence = 14> Accessed 03.04.16.

MacMillan, A., & Huff, B. (2009). *Transforming infoglut! A pragmatic strategy for oracle enterprise content management, manage corporate-wide content and intellectual property*. United States of America: The McGraw-Hill Companies Inc.

McKemmish, S. (1997). Yesterday, today and tomorrow: A continuum of responsibility. In *Paper presented at the proceedings of the records management association of Australia 14th National Convention, RMAA, Perth*. Retrieved from <http://www.sims.monash.edu.au/research/rcrg/publications/recordscontinuum/smckp2> Accessed 11.01.06.

McKemmish, S. (2001). Placing records continuum theory and practice. *Archival Science*, *1*(4), 333—359.

Myburgh, S. (2005). Records management and archives: Finding common ground. *The Information Management Journal*, *39*(2), 24—29.

Reed, B. (2005a). Reading the records continuum: Interpretations and explorations. *Archives and Manuscripts*, *33*(1), 19—43.

Reed, B. (2005b). Records. In S. McKemmish, M. Piggot, B. Reed, & F. Upward (Eds.), *Archives: Recordkeep in society*. Wagga Wagga: Centre for Information Studies.

Svärd, P. (2011a). Information management strategies in two Swedish municipalities: Similarities with enterprise content management. In J. Douglas (Ed.), *iRMA information and records management annual 2010* (pp. 153–182). St Helens, Tasmania: RIM Professionals Australasia.

Svärd, P. (2011b). *The interface between enterprise content management and records management in changing organizations (Licentiate Degree)*. Härnösand: Mid Sweden University.

Svärd, P. (2014). Information and records management systems and the impact of information culture on the management of public information *PhD Thesis*. Amsterdam: University of Amsterdam. Retrieved from http://dare.uva.nl/document/2/140656 Accessed 03.04.16.

Upward, F. (2000). Modelling the continuum as paradigm shift in recordkeeping and archiving processes, and beyond—A personal reflection. *Records Management Journal*, *10*(3), 115–139.

Upward, F. (2009). *Structuring the records continuum—Part One: Postcustodial principles and properties*. Retrieved from <http://www.infotech.monash.edu.au/research/groups/rcrg/publications/recordscontinuum-fupp1.html> Accessed 16.01.13.

Yusof, Z. M., & Chell, R. W. (2000). The records life cycle: An inadequate concept for technology-generated records. *Information Development*, *16*(3), 135–141.

Differences and similarities between enterprise content management and records management

5

5.1 Introduction

This chapter presents the differences and similarities between enterprise content management (ECM) and records management (RM). As organizations struggle to deal with their digital information resources, it has become crucial to understand the implications of the solutions they deploy. Organizations have a tendency of investing in information management technologies, which are trendy other than beginning by asking the right questions about their information environment. Dorsey (2005) argued that 50–80% of information systems projects fail and he attributed this failure to the human tendency to hide the bad news as he put it. This is also confirmed by Qassim (n.d.) who put the failure rate at 70–80%. Organizations often hire consultants and purchase software instead of beginning with identifying their information needs. The author led a consultancy that evaluated two studies that had been written by two IT companies, and that wanted to sell an ECM solution to a local administration in Belgium. Though the solutions that were being proposed were sound, this local administration was not ready to embark on an ECM implementation project. This was because there were so many challenges on the ground that needed to be addressed before new information management systems could be implemented. Luckily enough the municipality took the evaluation seriously and it waited with the implementation process which could have been catastrophic.

Dorsey (2005) suggested that the only way we can make information management system projects to work is by using our heads to ask the right questions. He contended that successful information system projects require top management support, a sound methodology, and solid technical leadership with experience from past projects. Mancini (n.d.) presented eight factors for a successful content and records management implementation project and these include the following:

- building a business strategy and blueprint by identifying the critical success factors for the project, how these factors will be measured, and what the drivers will be;
- conducting a technology assessment and creating a blueprint;
- thinking through a governance structure and approach—formal and documented rules governing information;
- creating a roadmap and project plan;

Enterprise Content Management, Records Management and Information Culture Amidst e-Government Development.
DOI: http://dx.doi.org/10.1016/B978-0-08-100874-4.00005-3

- designing the plan to include design of user support and operational procedures, security design, and design of infrastructure management processes;
- deploying the plan and cycle through phases of assessment and improvement; and
- undertaking change management. Failure in the implementation of ECM and records management projects is not because of the technology but lack of change management.

5.2 The study on the information management strategies of the two Swedish municipalities

In order to establish the differences between the ECM and RM, the author undertook a comprehensive literature review on both information constructs as demonstrated in Chapters 2 and 3, Records Management; Enterprise Content Management. She also carried out a study on the information management strategies of two Swedish municipalities to establish whether ECM was a known phenomenon and if the information management strategies of the municipalities were similar to it. This study was carried out between May and June 2010, and examined the management of structured and unstructured information: business process analysis; enterprise architecture; information management systems; e-Government development and e-services; organizational changes; effective information management; collaboration; information dissemination; repurposing of information; information overload; knowledge capture; and long-term preservation of information. A total of 18 interview schedules were sent out by email and 17 responses were received. The targeted administrative managers who could not participate recommended a person they thought was suitable. The three people who were recommended were IT Strategists/information officers from municipality A. The study particularly focused on administrative managers because they can make decisions and hence institute change and, additionally, information and records management issues require top management support (Shepherd & Yeo, 2003).

5.3 The literature review results

The literature review confirmed that ECM is a relatively new area of research that has engaged primarily information system researchers and the technology industry while records management is an established field and practice that has occupied records managers/archivists. While records management focuses on records and their evidentiary value ECM focuses on the management of unstructured content, which includes documents, web pages, reports, audio files, video clips, project spaces, and shared disk drives. ECM has an enterprise-wide view and prescribes eight factors salient to the effective management of information; enterprise architecture, business process management, change management, collaboration, knowledge management, system integration, repurposing of information, and the life-cycle information management. These factors are presented in Chapter 3, Enterprise content management. There are international standards that aim to promote good records management practices. No ECM standards are extant. Records management systems have been used to maintain the quality of records, that is, their authenticity, reliability, integrity, and usability while ECM systems endeavor to manage and facilitate access to all an organization's content.

Table 5.1 presents the identified characteristics of ECM and RM that are based on the literature review that the author carried out (for reference, see Chapters 2 and 3, Records management; Enterprise content management, for details):

The literature review resulted in an identification of the eight ECM factors mentioned on the foregoing page. These factors are referred to by the ECM proponents as crucial to the successful implementation of an ECM solution in an organization (Glazer, Jenkins, & Schaper, 2005; Jenkins, Köhler, & Shackleton, 2006; MacMillan & Huff, 2009; vom Brocke et al., 2008).

5.4 The overlap between enterprise content management and the information management strategies of the two municipalities

The study findings revealed that there were similarities between ECM and the information management activities of the municipalities. The majority of those interviewed in the study were not aware of ECM as a concept. There were, however, a few who confirmed that the way information was being managed in the municipalities had some similarity with some of the ECM factors. The following informant, e.g., argued:

> *I partly think that we manage information as in the ECM strategy. We have different ways of handling our digital information in the different business systems that are closely connected to the different business activities but, I think we still miss a cross-organizational approach (Officer E9).*

The municipalities were required to handle their information and records according to the legal framework governing public information. Within the information management framework, they undertook work that was similar to the ECM prescribed factors. This included: change management, business process management, collaboration, repurposing of information, knowledge management, and system integration (see Table 5.2).

The municipalities undertook change management whenever new systems were implemented because they recognized that without training staff, there would be a high risk of underutilization or rejection of the new information systems. Training also enabled the employees to acquire the necessary skills required in this new environment. There was also an opposite view that claimed that lots of investments

Table 5.1 **Characteristics of ECM and records management**

Discipline	ECM	RM
	An emerging field and practice; a subfield of information systems for the computing disciplines.	Is an established field and practice.
	Engages information systems researchers and the IT industry.	Engages records managers and archivists, and the IT industry.
	Endeavors to bring all of an organization's unstructured content into a managed environment in order to promote information sharing, controlled access, retrievability, and archiving.	Aims to control the creation, receipt, maintenance, use, and disposition of records efficiently and systematically.
	Defined as an integrated approach (an initiative) to managing all of an organization's information content.	
Systems	Facilitate access to all the relevant information in an organization.	Used to manage records effectively by maintaining their authenticity, reliability, integrity, and usability and to improving the quality and coherence of processes.
Drivers	Driven by the need to meet the global collaboration needs of an organization's employees, customers, and partners through digital information content.	Driven by legislative requirements: underpins government accountability, freedom of information, and privacy legislation, protection of people's rights and entitlements, and the quality of the archival heritage.
	A convergence of document management, web content management, and digital asset management.	
	Claims to improve business process management; collaboration; change management; repurposing of information; knowledge	Takes care of risk management, knowledge sharing, and organizational efficiency.

(*Continued*)

Table 5.1 (Continued)

Discipline	ECM	RM
	management; system integration; enterprise architecture; and the management of information throughout its life cycle.	
Focus	Focuses on content.	Focuses on records that are differentiated from other types of information because of their evidentiary value.
Social and technical aspects	Has social and technical aspects.	Has a social and technical aspect.
Approach	Life-cycle view: active, semiactive, and retention or destruction.	Has a life-cycle, a records continuum perspective, and a view to long-term preservation.
Orientation	Technology oriented but it is also claimed that it is also about the people and processes.	Both technology oriented and analog.
Standards	ECM is based on quality assurance standards ISO 9001 and ISO 17025. In 2006, the need for increased interoperability among disparate ECM applications gave rise to an international standards organization called interoperable enterprise content management (iECM) consortium. The aim was to define standards and best practice.	Guided by international standards and best practice such as: • ISO 15489.1: 2002 Records management—General • ISO 15489.2: 2002 Records management—Guidelines • Open Archival Information System (OAIS ISO 14721:2002) • Standard for metadata ISO 23081; • Technical Report on Work Process Analysis for Records ISO/TR 26122:2008 • ISO 30300:2011 Management system for records.

were being made in new applications but less was spent on change management. The following administrative manager P7 was, e.g., of the view that:

> *I think that little money is invested in training sessions. Expensive applications are bought and then it is believed that things will work out automatically and that is not often the case.*

Table 5.2 Activities pursued by municipalities A and B similar to ECM

ECM factors	Records management factors	
	Municipality A	***Municipality B***
Change management	Engaged in change management.	Engaged in change management.
Business process management	Process work was ongoing and process owners had been appointed. Results had led to the standardization of case handling in one of the units and the merging of some units.	Process work was ongoing but not at the same level as in municipality A. Results in one of the units had led to rationalization of work, reduction in staff, and the merging of units.
Collaboration	Staff members collaborated around information but not in a systematic manner. A project that aimed to promote information sharing was being planned. The municipality had issues when it came to collaboration with other municipalities around innovative ideas that had not yet become official. This is because once this information was captured then it had to be made accessible in accordance with the Public Records Act.	Staff members collaborated around information but not in a systematic manner.
Repurposing of information	Consultation with old records and the archives was performed. Investments in a common repository had been made to facilitate information access, sharing, and traceability. The municipality had undertaken information modeling though it was not enterprise wide.	Consultation with old records and archives was performed. Investments had been made in a centralized registry function to facilitate readily access of records and traceability.
Knowledge management	Employee-to-employee transfer of knowledge was the norm. Two projects were underway to capture and to systematize knowledge management.	Employee-to-employee transfer of knowledge was the norm.
System integration	Had started thinking about system integration at the systems procurement stage.	Had started thinking about system integration at the systems procurement stage.

Work with business process analysis was being undertaken but it was being pursued at differing levels of maturity. Municipality A had done much more than municipality B. Municipality A had, e.g., appointed process owners to work with process analysis. It, however, lacked a common definition for business process management. One of the informants argued that they had an IT perspective, a business perspective, and an information management perspective. The challenge was to create a common understanding of the term. In municipality B, process analysis was still premature, but there was awareness of its importance.

Collaboration around information management issues was emerging, and municipality A had even engaged in information modeling in order to identify information needs. However, this information modeling was not done at an enterprise-wide level. In both municipalities, the archives function was not integrated with the rest of the core functions, but archives were looked upon as a place to send records that were no longer active or a place to keep the original records. This meant that information that was to be reused was kept in the information management systems or in the intermediate archives. The central archives were consulted for old records. Information officers/IT Strategist P1 contended that close collaboration between the records management function and information technology units would facilitate the management of information. Some of the informants said they collaborated with the archivists and others were of the opposite view. Administrative Manager P15 stated that they had a good dialogue with the archivist:

> *Yes, but we could be better at utilizing the competence that we have in that area. I think that we have over time had a relatively good dialogue.*

One of the informants in municipality A argued that the administrative staff ought to be made aware of the fact that they need the archivists during information planning. The following informants argued that:

> *The municipal archivist is not consulted as much as I would wish but he is being used more and more to structure up information, especially when it comes to how information is used in the business processes. This is meant to facilitate for the archives to manage it later (IT Strategist P8).*
>
> *The archivist is a very progressive person but I think he is in certain processes consulted quite late (Administrative Manager P16).*
>
> *The archivist is rarely consulted. I think he was involved in the procurement of the case and records management system in the steering group, but there are lots of other systems that are procured and used without his knowledge (IT Strategist P1).*
>
> *I cannot answer whether the expertise of the archivist is utilized (Administrative Manager P13).*
>
> *The municipality has not been good at utilizing the competence of the archival institution and the archivist. It is bad at utilizing that competence and letting the archivist be actively involved (IT Strategist P9)*

The interviews revealed that in municipality B, there was no collaboration between the IT Unit and the archivist. In both municipalities, processes of information systems acquisition excluded the archivists and sometimes members of the IT unit. This created an IT infrastructure with disparate information systems that further exacerbated the issue of long-term preservation since the municipalities had to deal with many systems. Since the archivists were not consulted during information planning, the issue of long-term preservation was often not put into consideration. Focus was put on the management of current information in order to create more efficient business processes. The studies revealed that projects aimed at improving business processes often lacked long-term preservation strategies and this could be clarified by the fact that the archival expertise was often left out of such projects. The different information systems served as temporary "digital archives." IT Strategist P1 argued that:

> *Our worst example is that in this municipality (A) there are three personnel salary systems of which two are "storage." One of them is active and is our personnel administration system but since the other two have not been archived or migrated then they are also kept. It is a heavy job.*

Municipality A was faced with the challenge of maintaining aging systems because there were no better replacements. Some systems were maintained because integration was difficult or the measures to migrate the information to new platforms were too expensive. In both municipalities, information was being repurposed by consulting old records or the archives. The fact that the municipalities did not have digital archives further complicated the proper re-use of information. This was an area that needed further development. The municipalities faced the challenge of knowledge management. There was no systematic way of managing the knowledge accumulated by long-term employees who had developed specialized knowledge. However, there was awareness of the need to establish a more developed system for knowledge capture. The following informant argued that:

> *Knowledge management is quite unstructured. In certain cases it is necessary to ensure that those who leave the organization for various reasons and have critical business information, that it is retained in the organization. Normally we do not do it but let the information disappear (Administrative manager P14).*

The current knowledge management approach required retiring or vacating officers to pass on knowledge by working side by side with their replacements. This facilitated the maintenance of knowledge in-house while the replacement was being trained. The time period was limited as it was costly to pay two salaries for one position. Information/IT Strategist P8 revealed that a retired employee had tentatively introduced the idea of managing knowledge via a wiki. She further argued that this would be a systematic way to capture knowledge, but it would also require the engagement of all employees to document their problem solving tactics. In another instance, Administrative manager P12 expressed the fact that a project was being conducted to document the experiences of a member of staff who had worked in Municipality A for a long time. The project was to also include important documentation that has been accumulated by the retiring member of staff over the years. The project was to be completed before the person's retirement.

The issue of disparate information systems was caused by uncoordinated procurement processes that were done outside the formal procurement procedures, and lack of enterprise architecture to guide investments in the IT infrastructure. This resulted in an IT infrastructure with disparate systems that created islands of information. These systems became stand-alone systems and created inefficiency, duplication of information, and needed separate maintenance. This further created integration problems. There was, however, a realization in both municipalities of the necessity to create a more consolidated IT environment with integrated systems. Municipality A had, therefore, invested in a case and records management system and it needed to integrate all its information systems and to migrate information from these legacy systems. However, some of the information systems were very old which made it practically impossible. Some of the information was manually moved to the new systems, which was a time-consuming exercise. Municipality A had about 50 systems that were old, and if anything were to go wrong information would be lost. The management of unstructured data in both municipalities remained a challenge. Issues regarding enterprise architecture had become more pronounced in municipality A because there was a growing awareness of how information systems and business processes should be aligned. However, this alignment was not yet well planned for or mapped. Sometimes, individual units purchased small systems that were specific for their activities. The following informant argued:

> *The municipality has an IT plan which lays out the process for acquisition of new systems but since all departments have their own budgets and finance their own IT systems then one ignores the IT-plan and indeed they do (IT strategist P1).*

The information systems procurement process was supposed to involve representatives from different units, to establish whether an information system could serve more than one administrative unit. However, since the purchase of new systems was uncoordinated and was based on the individual administrative unit's needs, it led to the implementation of specialized systems that only a few people could manage. Administrative manager P3 argued that:

> *We have some obvious worries where we are supposed to collaborate beyond the information systems' boundaries. Right now we are in a process of changing the personnel system and the personnel planning system that are not integrated with each other. This is an area that needs further development. We have many specialized systems that are isolated.*

Specialized systems required special competence which made the municipalities vulnerable where personnel who managed them on a regular basis were absent from work. The management of different information systems was costly and posed challenges. Responding to the issue of system integration Administrative manager P5 and IT strategist P1 expressed the fact that:

> *Integration is a requirement but I cannot say it is an issue we have effectively dealt with. We still have one or two systems that appear without consultation (Administrative manager P5).*
>
> *The integration of systems is not thought about and when one buys new systems it comes up as a surprise during the pursuit of a project (IT strategist P1).*

An informant in Municipality A argued that they were instead faced with the problem of multiple integrations of systems that are not standardized, and had problems with upgrades. The acquisition and mergers of system suppliers also caused problems to the municipalities. This complication was often overlooked during the formulation of requirements specifications. This meant that once a supplier of a system was bought up by another company, then the maintenance of the supplied system could not be guaranteed. Municipality A, e.g., was forced to buy a new personnel system despite the fact that the system it was using was still new and functioned well. The personnel also had just been trained after its implementation and were acquainted with it. The municipalities were, despite the challenges of information management, engaging in e-Government development and hence transforming their way of working.

5.5 Conclusion

ECM like records management endeavors to help organizations to manage their information assets. The biggest difference between the two strategies is that while ECM focuses on content, records management focuses on records. Records management ensures that the records' evidential value, reliability, and authenticity are maintained. By focusing on content, ECM ensures that the information that falls outside the managed records is also brought into a managed environment and leveraged in a manner that supports business activities. In the case studies, it was evident that the focus was on current records captured in records management systems, but information in general information systems was neglected. The efforts that the municipalities were investing in information management were fragmentary and hence did not promote an enterprise-wide information management approach. The municipalities had records management functions and/or information management strategies. The research findings confirmed that the municipalities were also working with certain aspects of ECM. The maturity level of the ECM prescribed factors was however still low, and there were varying degrees of engagement in each of the municipalities. Both municipalities were engaged in business process analysis even though in Municipality B this was still a very premature engagement. They had also started discussing ways of collaborating around information in order to develop a culture of sharing it. They further discussed information reuse even though it was not done systematically. The municipalities still have much progress to make before they can be said to be reusing information in any meaningful way. This is due in part to the fact that reuse of information also requires an IT infrastructure that enables systems to at least interface with each other. As such, the municipalities had realized the need to address issues of system integration.

Despite these differences, the study showed that there were areas of overlap, or commonality, between ECM and the information management strategies of the municipalities. The overlap included: business process management; collaboration; change management; repurposing of information; knowledge management; system integration; and the life-cycle management of information. This overlap demonstrated the relevancy of the ECM factors and could within the municipalities information management framework lead to more awareness regarding what ought to be done, in order to achieve effective information management regimes. The Swedish municipalities still had to address the silo organizational structures, lack of top management support during the execution of projects, system integration, knowledge management, long-term preservation strategies, and resistance to change. Even though the municipalities had started engaging in the analysis of their business processes and were aware of the need for system integration, lack of enterprise architecture made the integration of information systems difficult.

ECM and records management differed primarily in five ways:

- ECM is an emerging field that requires further investigation, while records management is an established practice that continues to develop in order to devise tools to fit the current digital information management environment.
- ECM focuses on content that is all unstructured information in an organization, while records management focuses on records.
- ECM is driven by business efficiency while records management is in addition driven by legislation and broad societal needs. It promotes government efficiency, transparency, and accountability for democratic developments and enhances the societal memory.
- ECM is pursued by information systems scientists and the IT industry while records management has occupied records managers/archivists and the IT industry.
- ECM is technology-oriented while records management is both technology-oriented and analogue.

The study confirmed that there were also similarities as demonstrated in Table 5.2. These similarities, which covered areas of improvements pursued by the two municipalities, included:

- change management efforts conducted during the introduction of new systems;
- business process management undertaken to improve service delivery to the citizens;
- collaboration around information issues, which is still underdeveloped but is being discussed;
- system integration: an issue caused by lack of consultation and respect of information systems, procurement procedures; and
- both ECM and RM constitute the people, processes, and technology.

References

Dorsey, P. (2005). Top 10 reasons why systems projects fail. Retrieved from <http://www.ksg.harvard.edu/m-rcbg/ethiopia/Publications/Top%2010%20Reasons%20Why%20Systems%20Projects%20Fail.pdf> Accessed 26.04.16.

Glazer, D., Jenkins, T., & Schaper, H. (2005). *Turning content into competitive advantage, enterprise content management technology, what you need to know*. Ontario: Open Text Corporation.

Jenkins, T., Köhler, W., & Shackleton, J. (2006). *Turning content into competitive advantage, enterprise content management methods, what you need to now*. Ontario: Open Text Corporation.

MacMillan, A., & Huff, B. (2009). *Transforming Infoglut! A pragmatic strategy for oracle enterprise content management, manage corporate-wide content and intellectural property*. United States of America: The McGraw-Hill Companies Inc.

Mancini, J. (n.d.). 8 Secrets of an effective content or records management implementation. Retrieved from: <http://www.aiim.org/~/media/Files/8Things/8-Secrets-of-Content-and-Records-Management-Strategy.pdf> Accessed 26.04.15.

Qassim, A. A. (n.d.). Why information systems projects fail: guidelines for successful OMAN projects. Retrieved from <http://www.intosaiitaudit.org/intoit_articles/26_p12top17.pdf> Accessed 26.04.16.

Shepherd, E., & Yeo, G. (2003). *Managing records—a handbook of principles and practice*. London: Facet publishing.

vom Brocke, J., Derungs, R., Ivoclar, V., Herbst, A., Novotny, S., & Simons, A. (2008). The drivers behind enterprise content management: a process-oriented perspective (pp. 1–12). Retrieved from <http://is2.lse.ac.uk/asp/aspecis/20110037.pdf> Accessed 6.10.11.

Appendix A Interview guide—The study on the information management strategies of the municipalities

The purpose of this interview guide is to elicit responses regarding Enterprise Content Management (ECM) as a new information management construct. The data that will be collected will enable me to establish whether the information management strategies that the municipalities are using are the same or similar to ECM. The interview will be 45 min long and upon consent of the participant, it will be recorded. The interviews will only be used for research purposes.

A.1 The management of structured and unstructured information

Enterprise Content Management (ECM) is defined "as the technologies used to capture, manage, store, preserve, and deliver content and documents related to organizational processes. ECM tools and strategies allow the management of an organization's unstructured information, wherever that information exists" (Macmillan and Huff, 2009, p. 4). ECM is now being used in the private sector to manage both structured and unstructured information.

1.1 Have you heard about ECM before?
1.2 If yes, can you kindly explain to me what your understanding of ECM is?
1.3 Has ECM been implemented at your unit? If yes, how has it been implemented? If no, are there plans for its implementation?

A.2 ECM is closely linked to business process analysis (Macmillan and Huff, 2009; Butler Group, 2003). In order to identify relevant information, the processes that generate it need to be identified

2.1 Has your unit ever undertaken a process identification exercise?
2.2 If so, what processes were identified?
2.3 How were the personnel involved in the process mapping exercise?
2.4 What information and records were identified based on the process mapping exercise?
2.5 Was the unstructured information identified as important for the management of the unit activities?

A.3 Information management systems and enterprise architecture

It is argued in the literature on ECM that the acquisition and operation of information systems should be based on Enterprise Architecture in order to achieve effective information management through the integration and interoperability of the systems (Butler Group, 2005; Johnson and Ekstedt, 2007).

3.1 Does the municipality have enterprise architecture in order to identify technological needs and to facilitate integration and interoperability of systems?
3.2 What is the procedure for the acquisition of information systems in your unit?
3.3 Are issues of integration discussed prior to the acquisition of new systems?
3.4 How is the IT-unit involved in this process?
3.5 Do you have a systems coordinator at the unit?
3.6 How are the systems at your unit integrated with the rest of the systems within the municipality?
3.7 How are the information systems aligned with the business requirements of your unit?
3.8 What are the problems posed by stand-alone systems and how has your unit dealt with the challenges?

A.4 E-Government and e-services have meant increased transparency, accountability, and interaction with the citizens through information made available via government agencies' websites (Navarra and Cornford, 2005)

4.1 What is your opinion regarding this statement?
4.2 To what extent is your unit engaged in e-Government and what e-services does it deliver to the citizens?
4.3 How is the information that is generated by the e-services managed?
4.4 What are the policies applied to the management of this information?
4.5 What are the challenges that are posed by the management of this information?
4.6 How does the web-based information match the information that the unit offers the general public using other channels such as brochures, the telephone, physical interaction with the citizens?

A.5 Organizational changes

5.1 What organizational changes has the municipality undergone in order to meet with the current demands of high quality service delivery through the effective management of information?
5.2 How has this affected the organizational structures that existed before the changes were undertaken?
5.3 What improvements have been achieved?
5.4 Has your unit undertaken any change management? If yes, how was it carried out and what did it involve?
5.5 How was it perceived by the employees and how did you manage it?

A.6 Effective information management aims to elevate efficiency, enable organizations to meet with compliance and to deliver quality services. These are some of the reasons behind the ECM initiative

6.1 What is your understanding of effective information management?
6.2 What are the rules and regulations that govern the management of information in your unit?
6.3 To what extent does your unit comply with the rules and regulations that govern the management of information like the Public Access and Privacy Acts?
6.4 What are the measures that your unit undertakes to meet with compliance issues?
6.5 What measures has your unit put in place to guarantee information security?
6.6 Are the personnel aware of these security measures?

A.7 Collaboration and information dissemination

ECM builds on collaboration and therefore encourages information sharing (MacMillan and Huff, 2009).

7.1 Is information sharing encouraged?
7.2 How does your unit collaborate around information issues?
7.3 Is there a culture to share and disseminate information beyond your unit?

A.8 Repurposing of information

ECM aims to enable organizations to be able to reuse and evaluate the content in their possession in order to become cost effective (Rockley et al., 2003).

8.1 How is information reused or repurposed?
8.2 What measures are in place to enable the reuse of information?
8.3 Has your unit ever undertaken an evaluation of its content?

A.9 Information overload

9.1 Does your unit experience any information overload?
9.2 If yes, is the information overload from within the organization or from the general public?
9.3 How does the current information overload affect access to information both internally and by the general public?

A.10 Knowledge capture is an important aspect of the ECM strategy and this might be of great disadvantage when employees retire or leave

10.1 How is knowledge captured within your unit?
10.2 How is it shared?

A.11 Long-term preservation of information

The management of digital information requires long-term strategies if it is to be made available over time. The capture of both structured and unstructured digital information will pose challenges of dealing with the different formats.

11.1 What is your understanding of the challenges of long-term preservation of information in the systems your unit uses?

11.2 Are the challenges of managing digital information over time discussed before the acquisition of the information systems?
11.3 What policies are in place regarding the long-term preservation of information?
11.4 Is the expertise of the municipal Archivist consulted to ensure that plans are instituted to manage information over time, should the information systems become obsolete?

(2010.04.01)

Interview Participants' Coding

Table of participant codes		
Participant code	**Municipality**	**Role**
P1	A	Information/IT Strategist
P2	A	Administrative Manager
P3	A	Information/IT Strategist
P4	B	Administrative Manager
P5	B	Administrative Manager
P6	B	Administrative Manager
P7	B	Administrative Manager
P8	A	Administrative Manager
P9	A	Information/IT Strategist
P10	A	Administrative Manager
P11	A	Administrative Manager
P12	A	Administrative Manager
P13	A	Administrative Manager
P14	A	Administrative Manager
P15	A	Administrative Manager
P16	A	Administrative Manager

Information culture

6

6.1 Introduction

As an Information Scientist conducting research within the discipline of Archives and Information Science, I am always met with a lack of understanding of the type of research I engage in, especially when I mention my discipline. Though people understand what transparency and accountability is, the connection is rarely made to the importance of good information management practices. I, e.g., happened to get into a discussion with a quite renowned professor as she asked me what my postdoctoral research was focusing on and I replied, "truth commissions." The professor wondered what an information scientist had to do with truth commissions that are only concerned with excavating the truth! I could not resist asking how the truth is excavated, captured, and then relayed to society! This anecdote resonates with many people in the information management profession. Most creators of information rarely understand or worry about the information they create and are also quite unaware of the information management activities that are a result of the processes they engage in. We currently work in an information environment where we are all information creators and, therefore, information management challenges should be of concern to all people in an organization and the society at large.

Information technologies have also become a challenge to good and accountable information management since, they are often considered the solution to challenges in the digital information environment, leaving out the people issues. Since we have all become now all information creators, there seems to be an assumption that we all understand how to manage the information we create. This has meant that organizational employees are not given training in the management of information (Svärd, 2014). Information is created, managed, and used by people and it is, therefore, the activities of an organization's employees that enhance its effective management. This means that organizations face organizational, technical and cultural problems (Asproth, 2007). The organizational and technical problems have been explored by researchers such as Asproth, 2007; Asproth, Borglund, Samuelsson, & Öberg, 2010; McLeod, Childs, & Hardiman, 2010. However, the cultural issues have not received equally as much attention (Choo, Chun, Furness, Paquette, & Van den Berg, 2006; Douglas, 2010; Oliver, 2008; Svärd, 2014). Furthermore, a lot of knowledge that would improve the information culture of organizations has been produced, e.g., within the records management community to promote best practice and to mitigate information management challenges (Bearman, 1994; Dollar, 2000; Duranti & Preston, 2008; Duranti & Thibodeau, 2006; McLeod et al., 2010; R. McLeod & Shipman, 2010; Shepherd & Yeo, 2003) but all this research does not seem to be well diffused in the environments in which organizations operate.

Enterprise Content Management, Records Management and Information Culture Amidst e-Government Development.
DOI: http://dx.doi.org/10.1016/B978-0-08-100874-4.00006-5

Having worked with information management issues in a government institution, I comprehend what it means to implement good information and records management strategies and policies, in an environment where top management does not fully understand what one's role is. Without the support of top management, it becomes very hard for the rest of the organizational employees to respect the policies governing the information they create. It is this lack of understanding of the work that information management professionals do that partly creates the chaotic information management environments that organizations operate in today. The people issues are: predominant, fundamental, and challenging, and they concern culture, philosophical attitudes, lack of awareness of records management and electronic records management issues, knowledge, and skills (McLeod, Childs, & Hardiman, 2011). This is why authors such as Shepherd and Yeo (2003) argued that the analysis of an organization's culture may help information professionals to understand why an organization operates the way it does. The attitudes and norms are embedded in the type of culture that is espoused by an organization.

Culture is variably defined and Buch and Wetzel (2001, p. 40) defined culture as "a pattern of shared basic assumptions that the group learned as it solved its problems of external adaptation and internal integration, that has worked well enough to be considered valid and, therefore, to be taught to new members as the correct way to perceive, think, and feel in relation to those problems." Seel (2000) looked upon culture as the daily conversations and negotiations that take place among organizational members and which are directed at finding the proper way of doing things and deriving meaning from the surrounding environment. Alvesson (2002) posited that a cultural perspective facilitates a better understanding of organizations and defines culture as the setting in which behavior, social events, institutions, and process take place and are understood. The cultural dimension is, therefore, central to aspects of organizational life. He was of the view that the centrality of culture as a concept comes from shared meanings and that organizations are systems of shared meanings. Therefore, the beliefs held in common reduce misunderstandings and wrong interpretations of meanings. Hofstede (2001, p. 9) provided an anthropologically agreed on definition of culture as, "patterned ways of thinking, feeling and reacting, acquired and transmitted mainly by symbols, constituting the distinctive achievements of human groups, including their embodiments in artifacts; the essential core of culture consists of traditional (i.e., historically derived and selected) ideas and especially their attached values." Therefore, the type of culture espoused by an organization towards the management of information impacts the way organizational members value it.

Grimshaw (1995) posited in her report that human resources were key elements to an organization and its culture and that if organizations were to maximize their use, information flow and communication had to be well organized. The report further confirmed that information culture is part of corporate culture and that it is influenced by information. The use of information within an organization reflects the organizational and management style, which dictates whether information seeking and use is an individual or organizational activity. Grimshaw argued that an organization's culture may be entrepreneurial, conservative, familial, and individualistic, led, managed, ethical or amoral.

A lot of focus has been put on information technology and yet, better computers and communication networks do not necessarily lead to better information environments. Davenport (1997) therefore proposed the term information ecology, which puts a narrow focus on technology, but addresses the way people create, distribute, understand, and use information. He argued that information ecology requires new management frameworks, incentives and attitudes toward organization hierarchy, complexity, and division of resources (Davenport, 1997). According to Davenport, ecology is the science of understanding and managing whole environments. He was against the modeling of information environments on machines and buildings and preferred living things. He defined information ecology as "holistic management of information" or "human-centered information management" (Davenport, 1997, p. 11). This kind of thinking puts humans at the center of the information world and technology on the periphery. He believed that ecological approaches to information management were more modest, behavioral and practical compared to the grand designs of information architecture and machine engineering. Six years after Davenport's argument against the focus on information technology as a solution to information management issues, Curry and Moore (2003) also concluded that the adoption of information technology alone is not sufficient. To deliver effective information management, information technology has to be complemented with a good information culture. Therefore, in order to achieve good information management practices, organizations need to have the employees at the centre of the information management solutions.

The political, administrative, and technological challenges have affected information management practices and hence brought about new requirements on the creation and management of information (Svärd, 2014). Organizations are therefore constantly undergoing change and this may stimulate the creation of different cultures. Whether an organization is public or private, it has to espouse competition, co-operation, loyalty, and trust and employee welfare. These developments are giving rise to complex cultures (Shepherd & Yeo, 2003).

6.2 Definitions of information culture

Information culture is defined differently as demonstrated in the examples that follow. Davenport (1997) defined information culture as the pattern of behaviors and attitudes that express an organization's orientation toward information. He contended that information cultures can be open, closed, factually oriented or rumor and intuition-based, controlling or empowering and internally or externally focused. Authors such as Choo et al. (2006) defined information culture as the organization's values, norms, and practices toward the management and use of information. The values and norms are perceived as follows:

- The values provide answers to what the organization perceives to be the role and contribution of information to organizational effectiveness and what values underlie the organizational style of managing its creation and use of information.

- Norms are derived from values and are socially accepted rules or standards that define what is normal or to be expected in the organizations. They can be informal or formal. Informal norms and attitudes influence the creation, flow, and use of information in individuals or groups. Formal rules, routines and polices are meant to plan, guide, and control information as an asset in an organization.

Douglas defined information culture as "an emerging complex system of values, attitudes, and behaviors that influence how information is used in an organization. Information culture exists in the context of and is influenced by an organizational culture and the wider environment" (Douglas, 2010, p. 388). Douglas' definition captures the complexity of information culture. Her qualitative study explored the values, attitudes, beliefs, and behaviors that government departments in Western Australia showed toward information. Even though information was pervasive in all government departments, the value the departments ascribed to it and their attitudes and behavior toward it were not well understood. Her study found information culture to be complex, systemic, and reflexive. She also identified intricate relationships between information culture and organizational culture, information management and information use. Like Curry and Moore (2003), she asserted that although information culture is frequently used as a concept, there is no agreed upon definition. Her research identified different types of information cultures that can be found in organizations and they include the following:

- Functional culture: managers use information as a means of exercising influence or power over others.
- Sharing culture: managers and employees trust each other to use information (especially about problems and failures) to improve their performance.
- Inquiry culture: managers and employees search for information to better understand the future and ways of changing what they do to align themselves with future trends/directions.
- Discovery culture: managers and employees are open to new insights about crisis and radical changes and seek ways to create competitive discontinuities (Douglas, 2010, p. 48).

Douglas (2010) highlighted paucity of studies on information culture yet it is supposed to give organizations a competitive advantage, if well aligned with business strategies. Widén-Wulff (2000) was of the view that information culture is about information systems, common knowledge, and individual information systems in form of attitudes and information ethics. She concluded that the organizations she reviewed were aware of the importance of information, but argued that it was the most difficult asset to manage (Widén-Wulff, 2000).

The connection between information culture and organizational culture was also confirmed by Curry and Moore (2003), who used organizational culture as a starting point for their research on information management in healthcare. Finding it difficult to quantify and qualify culture and information, they discussed the need for a tool to measure and develop an information culture. They posited that it requires a well-developed organizational culture if information culture is to be nourished. This further clarifies why information culture and organizational culture are intertwined. The two concepts have common attributes in the form of values, assumptions, and beliefs. They defined information culture as "A culture in which the value and utility of information in achieving operational and strategic success is recognized, where information forms the basis of organizational decision making and Information Technology is readily exploited as an enabler for effective Information Systems" (Curry & Moore, 2003, p. 94). Oliver (2011) also posited that information culture is inextricably linked to organizational culture and that the term connotes cultural characteristics that are unique to a particular organization.

Choo, Bergeron, Detior, and Heaton (2008) have also argued that information culture and organizational culture are an integral part of a process of becoming a knowledge-based organization. Seel (2000, p. 2) posited that "Organization culture is the emergent result of the continuing negotiations about values, meanings, and proprieties between the members of that organization and with its environment." Oliver (2004, 2008) contended that information culture exists in all organizations. An effective information culture requires effective communication flows, cross-organizational partnerships, cooperative working practices, and open access to relevant information, management of information systems, clear guidelines and documentation for information and data management, trust, and willingness to share information. Information culture could also be stable beliefs that constitute assumptions, values, norms, and attitudes. It encompasses behaviors, such as work practices, rituals, social dramas, and communication (Travica, 2008). Travica was of the view that information culture is that part of organizational culture that evolves around information and IT and that it is these two elements that shape the culture of an organization. Examples of cultural attitudes include preferences for facts or rumors, information behaviors that include information sharing, and the choice of communication channels.

Choo, Bergeron, et al. (2008) established whether there is a systematic way to identify the information behaviors and values that characterize an organization's information culture. Amongst the influences they found and that shape the information culture of an organization are: mission, history, leadership, employee traits, industry and national culture. Again they asserted, that information culture as a concept has not been adequately explored in current research. The results of their 2006 research demonstrated that different organizational issues need to be effectively managed if information is to be leveraged in a manner that gives a competitive advantage.

6.3 Information culture models and typologies

All organizations have models of information governance, which are referred to as political systems (Davenport, 1997). These models form local or centralized control of information management. In order to be able to establish the governing information management model in an organization, Davenport's research outlined the following models:

- Information federalism: based on consensus and negotiation on organization's key information elements and reporting structures.
- Information feudalism: individual business units manage own information, define own needs and report only limited information to the overall organization.
- Information monarchy: information categories and reporting structures defined by firm's leaders may or may not share information after collecting it.
- Information anarchy: absence of any overall information management policy, individuals obtain and manage own information.

Choo (2013) developed a typology of information culture, which includes the following:

- A result: oriented culture, where the goal of information management is to enable the organization to compete and succeed in its market or section.
- A rule: following culture where information is managed to enable the organization to control internal operations and to reinforce rules and policies.
- A relationship-based culture, where information management aims to encourage communication, participation and a sense of identity.
- In a risk-taking culture, where information is managed to encourage innovation, creativity, and exploration of new ideas.

The result-oriented culture pursues goal achievement and competitive advantage, the rule-following culture pursues control, compliance, and accountability, the relationship-based culture pursues communication, commitment, and participation, and the risk taking culture pursues innovation, exploration of new ideas and creativity. He postulated that organizations can display, to varying degrees, norms and behaviors from all the four information culture types. He concluded that identifying an organization's culture would facilitate cultural change and hence a systematic implementation of change.

Using a ministry with an informal training records management program, Wright (2013) interviewed 207 employees and explored Curry's and Moore's information culture assessment tool. She examined information culture in a regulated government environment. Her aim was to establish the relationship between records management training provided to staff, staff self-perceptions of records, management competencies and compliance with a formal records management program. She concluded that there is a correlation between formal training delivered to staff and the self-perceived level of records management competency. This means that the more training that the staff get, the more they perceive the need for further training in order to achieve the level of compliance required by the records management program. She was also of the view that understanding information culture features is crucial to the identification of gaps in dealing with the challenges of organizational records management training and the effect it has on compliance with organizational information and records management programs.

The table below is based on a literature review that the author conducted and presents components of information culture, information models, and a framework for the assessment of information culture, effective culture requirements, and the different types of culture as identified by the presented authors. The author does not claim that the table is exhaustive:

Components of information culture (Choo et al., 2008)	**Information models and framework by Curry & Moore, 2003; Davenport, 1997; Oliver, 2011**	**Types of culture (Douglas, 2010, p. 48)**
Communication flows—the importance of effective organizational communication cannot be overstated. Cross-organizational partnerships—this relates to organizational synergy and how different. functions and departments work together. Internal environment (cooperativeness, openness, and trust)—arguably the greatest influence on organizational culture is people. An Information culture requires cooperative working practices and open access to relevant information where applicable. Information systems management—the IS strategy needs to be closely linked to the business strategy with IT as the enabler of computerized IS. Information management. The enthusiasm, support. Cooperation of key personnel are indispensable elements of a successful information culture. Processes and procedures—the concise and clear documentation of key policies, processes, and procedures within an organization are an indicator of culture.	**Davenport's Model:** *Information federalism* is based on consensus and negotiation on organization's key information elements and reporting structures. *Information feudalism* is how individual business units manage own information, define own needs, and report only limited information to the overall organization. *Information monarchy* is where information categories and reporting structures defined by firm's leaders may or may not share information after collecting it. *Information anarchy* is the absence of any overall information management policy; individuals obtain and manage own information. **Curry and Moore's Model:** Effective communication flows. Cross-organizational partnerships. Cooperative working practices and open access to relevant information. Management of information systems. Clear guidelines and documentation for information and data management.	Functional culture is when managers use information as a means of exercising influence or power over others. Sharing culture is when managers and employees trust each other to use information (especially about problems and failures) to improve their performance. Inquiry culture is when managers and employees search for information to better understand the future and ways of changing what they do to align themselves with future trends/direction. Discovery culture is when managers and employees are open to new insights about crisis and radical changes and seek ways to create competitive discontinuities.

Components of information culture (Choo et al., 2008)	Information models and framework by Curry & Moore, 2003; Davenport, 1997; Oliver, 2011	Types of culture (Douglas, 2010, p. 48)
	Trust and willingness to share information. **Oliver's Information Culture Framework (ICF)** *Level one:* Is the fundamental layer of an organization's information culture and it includes: – respect for information as evidence; – respect for information as knowledge; – willingness to share information; – trust in information; – language requirements; and – regional technological infrastructure. *Level two:* Skills, knowledge, and experience related to information management, which can be acquired and/or extended in the workplace: – Information-related competencies, including information and computer literacy. – Awareness of environmental (societal and organizational) requirements relating to information. *Level three:* The third and uppermost layer is reflected in: – The information governance model that is in place. – Trust in organizational systems.	

6.4 Information culture and business success

Organizations are drowning in information that flows in from different channels. They hence need the ability to effectively manage it as knowledge and this is a prerequisite for innovativeness and business success (Widén-Wulff, 2000). As early as 1993, Ginman wondered how access and the utilization of information could be improved to lead to successful business. She concluded that the answer could be found in the identification of the characteristics of positive information cultures and their implementation according to the needs of the organization. Information is defined as part of corporate culture and a corporate culture that emphasizes information issues is related to positive company performance (Höglund, 1998). For organizations to achieve superior business performance, Choo et al. (2006, p. 494) argued that they must have the following capabilities:

- Information technology practices: the capability to effectively manage IT applications and infrastructure to support operations, business processes, innovation, and managerial decision making.
- Information management practices: the capacity to manage information effectively over the life cycle of information use, including sensing, collecting, organizing, processing, and maintaining information.
- Information behaviors and values: the capability to instill and promote behaviors and values in people for effective use of information.

Widén-Wulff (2000) was of the view that many professionals, policy makers, and managers lack a proper understanding of the role of information management, technologies, and knowledge sharing as causes, catalysts, facilitators, and obstacles in a work place. Though information management has been a domain of the IT departments, today's information landscape requires the engagement of top management because it is no longer just a technological issue. The competitive business environment requires access to timely and high-quality information and this hinges on well-designed information management governance models. The quality of information affects decision-making processes and, therefore, top management has the responsibility to define the information needed to run the business successfully (Tieto Corporation, 2013).

6.5 Exploring information culture using the Information Culture Framework (ICF)

This section presents a summary of results from a study that the author carried out on information culture in three municipalities, two in Sweden, and one in Belgium in September and November, 2012, respectively. The study entailed conducting interviews in the municipalities in order to access the norms, attitudes, and the value the municipal employees had towards the management of public records. A total of 54 interviews were conducted: 21 in Belgium and 33 in the two Swedish municipalities. The categories of people interviewed included heads of departments, heads of units, architects, environmental officers, geographical information system (GIS) managers, secretaries, building permit granting officers, an archivist, archives assistants, registrars, a receptionist, and social workers. The full study is presented in the author's PhD thesis entitled *Information and Records Management Systems and the Impact of Information Culture on the Management of Public Information*, 2014. The Swedish municipalities were referred to as A and B and the Belgian municipality as C. Oliver's (2011) Information Culture Framework (ICF) was modified and used to explore the type of information culture that the municipalities espoused. It constitutes three levels as follows (Table 6.1):

Table 6.1 Oliver's Information Culture Framework

Level one	The fundamental layer of an organization's information culture includes: • respect for information as evidence; • respect for information as knowledge; • willingness to share information; • trust in information; • language requirements; and • regional technological infrastructure.
Level two	Skills, knowledge, and experience related to information management, which can be acquired and/or extended in the workplace: • Information-related competencies, including information and computer literacy. • Awareness of environmental (societal and organizational) requirements relating to information.
Level three	The third and uppermost layer is reflected in: • the information governance model that is in place and • trust in organizational systems.

Source: Oliver, G. (2011). *Organizational culture for information managers*. Oxford: Chandos Publishing, pp. 126–127.

For the purpose of the study, the author modified Oliver's model because all its components were not relevant to the study of the municipalities. The author, therefore, used the following modified model to pursue the objective of the study:

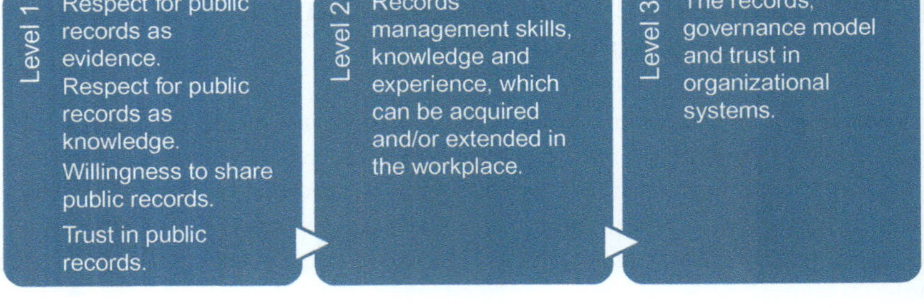

Source: Svärd, P. (2014). *Information and records management systems and the impact of information culture on the management of public information*. p. 23.

All the three municipalities deployed information and records management systems to facilitate the capture and management of information and records. The study focused on the management of records.

Level One: Respect for public records as knowledge; willingness to share information; and trust in public records:

The Swedish municipalities (A and B) had a registry function, which facilitated the pluralization of records, since they were organized and could be retrieved and made available upon request to different stakeholders. Municipalities A and B were sensitive to the management of public records and they exhibited respect for records. They had a culture that endeavored to take care of public records and the Swedish officers knew the laws governing public access to government records, and the specific laws that governed their respective areas of work. The Archives Act, which in detail describes and explains how government institutions should manage their records, was only known to the registrars and archives assistants, who acted as a link between the rest of the officers and the central archives.

The fact that the Swedish municipalities had a well-developed registry also meant that there was a systematic management of public records. This, however, did not mean that there were no challenges. Email management was still problematic, and it was expressed that some officers had problems in determining what emails constituted public records. In Sweden, email correspondence is not differentiated from traditional correspondence and hence should be managed in a similar manner (Gränström, Lundquist, & Fredriksson, 2000). The number of emails received a day also increased the risk of neglecting or deleting public records. However, email correspondence that was identified as public records was sent to the registry for registration. There were also paper records that were supposed to have been submitted to the central archives, but were still being kept at the departments. Municipality B experienced that the bulk of paper records had become difficult to use as a reference source.

The Swedish municipalities had qualified archivists, who were not so much involved in the management of current records. The registrars, who did not have the same level of education in records management and a holistic understanding of the entire records continuum like the archivists did, were more involved in the management of current records. They were hence in constant contact with the rest of the municipal officers. The registrars had only attended courses in the registration of public records and were said to be good at their work.

In the Belgian case study (case C), the capture, management, organization, and the pluralization of records was problematic since the registry function was underdeveloped. The respect shown towards the management of public records depended on how highly regulated the function of a particular department was. This conclusion was based on the information that some of the informants shared with the author. They emphasized that they could not afford to make mistakes and that there were a series of records that they had to maintain on file because lack of proper documentation had legal repercussions. However, lack of a fully developed registry function compromised the effective management of public records and made them difficult to trace. This further resulted in loss of time, since a good number of the employees, especially the newly recruited, spent most of their precious time looking for records. The officers' email boxes were according to the law private and hence beyond the records management function that took care of the municipality's records. Municipality C was, however, planning to develop e-services, which raises questions regarding the privatized email boxes. Most people communicate using email, but the informants confirmed that it was the paper record that was considered official.

In Municipality C, it was people who did not have records management training who were in charge of the active management of the records. The municipality had staff members who registered incoming public records, but they were not trained registrars. The archivist was again responsible for the management of the records that had to be sent to the archives. He was not actively involved in the management of the active records. This evidently caused problems as people instituted their own ways of managing records, and lack of a records management policy made the situation worse. The informants expressed frustration over the fact that they did not know what to with the records. Lack of records management policy made it hard to create, capture, organize, and to manage the generated records. The abscence of records management guidelines meant that important records were destroyed without consultation with the archivist. This kind of environment promoted inadequate records management behavior where some members of staff did not have respect for records.

Managing records for knowledge and information sharing was not fully developed in any of the three cases. The registries in municipalities A and B facilitated access, use, and reuse of records. A folder structure was also used to share information on the Intranet. Some of the information systems intended to facilitate knowledge management and information sharing posed integration challenges and instead created information islands. In municipality A, despite efforts to invest in an expensive system to create a common repository that would facilitate records management and hence foster knowledge and information sharing, some of the employees expressed frustration about the system. The intent was to integrate most of the information systems with the case and records management system, but this was not feasible. The system was to manage as many business processes as possible, but it had so far only facilitated the inclusion of one process. Municipality B had an integration problem too, which resulted in the double registration of public records and frustrated employees and, the system suppliers were not being very helpful.

Municipality C also faced systems integration problems and these were caused by the procurement process that was not coordinated. This frustrated the staff who decided to neglect the use of the records management system that had been put in place to facilitate, records capture, knowledge and information sharing. The system was implemented to capture records and to serve as a common repository but it was insufficient in functionality. The majority of those interviewed had developed a culture of not using the system it because they claimed it was not user-friendly.

Lack of consultation and collaboration around the procurement of information management systems in the three case studies led to an IT-infrastructure with disparate information systems. This did not promote information access and hindered the effective use of information.

As regards the management of records in all the three cases, most of the interviewed officers shared their experiences with each other. Consultations were made with those officers who were seen as "experts" in records management in the departments. However, the so-called experts were not experts in records management, but they knew the laws that governed their specific areas of work and the type of documentation that was required to be maintained. They did not have a holistic view of records management issues and easily brushed off questions that were beyond their understanding, as the responsibility of the archives. A Head of Unit in Municipality A argued that archives were still seen as a "museum" in his municipality, instead of regarding them as information banks to be actively used as per the continuum model. This kind of view was also prevalent in all the three case studies even though some of the participants consulted the archives on a regular basis, for reference purposes. The majority of the participants looked at archives as a place to preserve records for historical purposes only.

In the Swedish cases, despite the many years some of the officers had spent at their jobs, the management of public records was routine bound. Most of the interviewed officers had worked for the municipalities for many years and handled records as a matter of routine. There was a feeling that people knew what to do with public records. One of the archives assistants in Municipality B, however, wondered if some of the officers understood why they managed records the way they did. In other words, the management of records was something a person did because the law dictated so. Except in one case of a Unit Head, officers did not make reference to the fact that records were a tool for knowledge management, information sharing, and efficiency. Some of the experts were excluded from the early phases of the records management continuum and this is why improvements directed at the information management environment were fragmentary.

Level 2: Records management skills, knowledge, and experience, which can be acquired and/or extended in the work place:

The registrars in Municipality A had been offered a course for registrars and they also had attended courses for experienced registrars. Their head of unit confirmed that they were people who were experts in their area and had long experience since they had worked at other local administrations. However, they were not people with substantial university studies but had mostly received internal training. In case study B, it was the archival assistants and the registry staff who were referred to as the professionally trained records management officers, and the experts. However, one of the archives assistants confirmed that she did not feel so confident when it came to the laws governing public information or other records management issues. Her education background was basic. The second archives assistant did not even know whether she still had that role archives, because by the time the interviews were conduted, a new system was being introduced. Everybody was to get involved in the registration of public records. This was a new development that required officers to register the cases they handled directly into the system, instead of sending them to the registrars like the practice was. She had too undertaken a seven points university course in records management.

In Municipality C, the assistants who worked as the link between the business officers and the archives service were not qualified records assistants or managers. They had no records management background. The archives service took care of the records when they were no longer active. There was a big delay between the time of creation and the time when the archives service claimed the records. This created a state of anarchy where officers created their own systems. Most officers kept everything, which also created an information overload and made the search and use of records difficult.

Some of the informants in Municipalities A and B confessed that they could always become better, and that they would appreciate records management courses or sessions that would give them a deeper understanding of the laws governing the area. Doing things by routine is good, but in a changing world even those who have several years' experience can be challenged by the changes that sometimes take place in organizations. Some of the officers did not think they needed any records management training because they had worked for the municipalities for a long time and knew the procedures. However, they felt unsure when it came to the management of email correspondence. Further, the courses that were given to the staff responsible for records management were quite elementary in comparison with the current complex environment.

In the Belgian case, the informants lacked motivation to manage public records. Records were managed according to personalized systems and to facilitate the execution of one's work. This was not good for the organization, especially since the municipality recruited young people who moved on without structuring the information and the knowledge they created. This meant that newcomers had to sometimes start from scratch or waste a lot of their initial time figuring out what their predecessors had done. The informants confirmed that they were never offered any courses in records management. They expressed interest in a course that would foster a full understanding of records management. The informants felt very unsure when managing public records since the municipality did not have a records management policy and there were no guidelines to facilitate the management of public records. They expressed frustration over not knowing what they should do with the records.

In case C records management was not a prioritized issue by management and no courses were being offered to the municipal employees. One of the departmental heads, however, argued that improvements were being made and they were mostly being pushed by the archives service. He further opined that records management should have been an issue on the management agenda. The legal framework governing public records was only known to a few of the interviewed officers. The officers were expected to know the laws that governed the records that they generated. They however expected the archives service to let them know how long public records had to be maintained. This enormously affected the entire records management environment, since the insecurity felt by the officers made them keep "everything." "We keep everything" was a common phrase among the officers that the author interviewed. It automatically led to an information overload in the systems and hence overshadowed important information. It also made retrieval of records problematic. There was no records management policy except for the email policy, which was old and not known to the majority of the officers.

The research findings from all the three municipalities confirmed that records management was not regarded as a function that needed fully qualified personnel. Training was not prioritized and when it took place, it was often in conjunction with the implementation of a new information management systems. Records management was mostly done by routine and the officers confirmed that they consulted their fellow colleagues or immediate managers whom they looked upon as "experts." Though some informants were of the view that the management groups of the Swedish case studies did not prioritize records management a good majority confirmed that they did.

6.6 The records governance model and trust in organizational systems

Municipalities A and B had well-developed records and archives policies, but these were not known to some of the officers except in one case in Municipality B where a head of unit made reference to a handbook. There was a strong adherence to the legal framework that governs public records even though the Archives Act was not known. However, those working with records management confirmed that management trusted that they knew their job and that it was their responsibility to ensure that the legal framework was followed. There was also high trust in the use of the common systems put in place to manage records. The case and records management systems were seen as common repositories where one could access records.

In Municipality C the records governance model had many weaknesses. The structures that could have facilitated the capture and management of public records were not fully developed. The case and records management system that had been put in place to manage the registration of public records did not capture the entire records flow, that is the incoming and outgoing records. The officers did not show trust in their registry. They were expected to register and to access the records in the case and records management system. They instead created personalized systems due to fear that they would not be able to readily access their records since the system was not user-friendly. Others did not use the system because they had heard from fellow colleagues that they also did not use it. In Municipality C where the records governance model did not include a well-developed registry, public records were not being effectively captured. This also led to a culture where officers could choose not to use the records management system.

6.7 Conclusion

Research on information culture confirms a correlation between good information management practices and business efficiency. Despite the deployment of information systems, effective information management is still difficult to achieve. A lot of focus has been put on information management systems while research shows that the people issues are equally important and need to be addressed. People should be put at the centre of information management solutions. This is what Davenport (1997) referred to as information ecology. The fact that we are all information creators has still not endowed upon us the understanding required to manage information as a vital resource. Despite the fact that information is considered to be the fuel that drives organizations today, most people are yet to understand that it has to be strategically planned for and that information management is no longer only a only domain for records managers, archivists, and registrars. The information landscape today is complex and hence requires the involvement of all people in an organization and especially top management. It is about collaboration, if information is to be accessed readily across departmental boundaries and if information sharing is to be promoted. This further entails creating and promoting positive norms, attitudes, and values towards the creation, use, management, and reuse of information and records. Investments in information technology cannot alone lead to a positive information culture.

Furness et al. (2006) summed it up well by stating that in order for an organization to achieve superior business performance it must have capabilities in: information technology practices, information management practices and information behaviors and values. A negative information culture as the conducted studies proved develops, when people do not trust the information and records management systems put in place to facilitate the management of information. I have overused the deleted sentence!. This is when the employees develop their own personalized systems in order to have readily access to their documents. In organizations where top management shows little interest in information management issues, the rest of the organizational employees equally devotes less attention to the way they manage the information they produce. The Swedish municipalities demonstrated that having a well-functioning registry promoted positive information culture because organizational employees knew where to turn to when searching for records. They also regarded the registry as a common repository for their records, which facilitated knowledge sharing and the effective use of the registry system.

The people issues make it imperative to offer courses in information and records management to all organizational employees. This would create awareness about the need to effectively manage the information that is generated during the conduct of business processes, and hence lead to the development of a positive information culture. It is easier for people to engage if they have an understanding of why information, especially in the digital environment, has to be managed properly, from its creation, preservation, and reuse. The employees in the Belgian municipality hated records management because they lacked the skills to do it.

The Swedish municipalities had to a certain extent a more developed information culture even though it was not free from challenges. The biggest challenge was the management of electronic records, which requires a change in the paper-mindset that dominated, especially among personnel who had worked for the municipalities for several decades. The over confidence displayed by the Swedish officers towards the management of public records could also hinder the open mind required to understand the current information landscape and its complexities. In the Belgian case, lack of structures to facilitate the management of records was a big challenge. The municipality had many challenges in its records management environment and these included: lack of a fully developed registry, system integration, a records management policy, electronic archives, and the creation of personalized systems that led to the neglect of the common system put in place to manage records.

Where there was lack of respect for records, the records were not effectively captured. Lack of respect for records as sources of knowledge and information sharing tools, meant that it was difficult to share knowledge and information. Where skills to manage records were insufficient, the employees had negative experiences about records management. An underdeveloped records governance model in the Belgian case also meant lack of trust in the case and records management system that had been put in place to manage records. In such an environment, the employees did not embrace the solutions that were meant to achieve a positive information culture. Information culture, therefore, affects the factors that would create a well functioning information and records management infrastructure. It hence affects the capture, management, organization, and pluralization of public records.

In conclusion, information culture is an important part of information/records management in organizations because it is about the soft issues that are often overlooked, when searching for solutions to deal with the challenges in today's information landscape. In the researched municipalities, information culture influenced the factors that were meant to achieve good records management practices. This is because the attitudes of the employees and the way they understood and valued public records affected their management. This conclusion was based on the following:

- Where there were no formulated records management policies, the attitudes towards the management of public records were more relaxed. This created an anarchistic environment as stated in Davenport's model (1997) where employees created their own systems and managed the records as personal property. This made the capture, organization, management, and use of public records difficult.
- Lack of training in records management led to lack of an understanding as to why public records had to be managed according to certain criteria.
- Lack of collaboration affected information planning and led to the procurement of disparate information systems, which caused integration problems and a disparate IT infrastructure.

The outlined issues are people related and they have to do with the information culture of the organizations that the author researched. These are issues that can be dealt with in order to achieve a well-functioning information/records management infrastructure and to develop a positive information culture.

References

Alvesson, M. (2002). *Understanding organizational culture*. London: Sage Publications.

Asproth, V. (2007). Integrated information systems—A challenge for long-term digital preservation. *Interdisciplinary Journal of Information, Knowledge, and Management, 2*, 90–98.

Asproth, V., Borglund, E., Samuelsson, G., & Öberg, L. M. (2010). *E-tjänstens framtida historia - informationsbevarande, ett bortglömt ansvarsområde? I Förvaltning och medborgarskap i förändring. Red. Lindblad-Gidlund, Katarina, Ekelin, Annelie, Eriksén, Sara, Ranerup, Agneta*. Malmö: Holmbergs i Malmö AB.

Bearman, D. (1994). *Electronic evidence: Strategies for managing records in contemporary organizations*. Pittsburgh: Archives & Museum Informatics.

Buch, K., & Wetzel, D. K. (2001). Analyzing and realigning organizational culture. *Leadership & Organizational Development Journal, 22*(1), 40–43.

Choo, W. C., Bergeron, P., Detior, B., & Heaton, L. (2008). Information culture and information use: An exploratory study of three organizations. *Journal of the American Society for Information Science and Technology, 59*(5), 792–804.

Choo, C. W. (2013). Information culture and organization effectiveness. *International Journal of Information Management, 33*(5), 775–779.

Choo, W. C., Furness, C., Paquette, S., & Van den Berg, H. (2006). Working with Information: Information management and culture in a professional services organization. *Journal of Information Science, 32*(6), 491–510.

Curry, A., & Moore, C. (2003). Assessing information culture—An exploratory model. *International Journal of Information Management, 23*(2), 91–110.

Davenport, T. H. (1997). *Information ecology. Mastering the information and knowledge environment.*. Oxford: Oxford University Press.

Dollar, M. C. (2000). *Authentic electronic records: Strategies for long-term access*. Chicago, Illinois: Cohasset Associates, Inc.

Douglas, J. (2010). *The identification, development and application of information culture in the Western Australian public sector*. Western Australia: PhD Thesis, Faculty of Computing, Health and Science, Edith Cowan University.

Duranti, L. & Preston, R. (2008). International research on permanent authentic records in electronic systems (InterPARES 2), Experiential, interactive and dynamic records. Padova.

Duranti, L., & Thibodeau, K. (2006). The concept of record in interactive, experiential and dynamic environments: the view of InterPARES. *Archival Science, 6*, 13–68.

Ginman, M. (1993). Information culture and business performance. Åbo: Institution för biblioteksvetenskap och informatik.

Gränström, C., Lundquist, L., & Fredriksson, K. (2000). *Arkivlagen, bakgrund och kommentarer*. Göteborg: Graphic Systems AB, (Vol. andra upplagan,).

Grimshaw, A. (1995). *Information culture and business performance*. University of Hertfordshire Press, Hertfordshire.

Hofstede, G. (2001). *Cultures, consequences. comparing values, behaviors, institutions and organizations across nations* (2nd ed.). Thousand Oaks: Sage Publications.

Höglund, L. (1998). A case study of information culture and organizational climates. *Svensk Biblioteksförskning/Swedish Library Research, 3–4*, 73–86.

McLeod, J., Childs, S. & Hardiman, R. (2010). *The AC + erm project. Funded by the arts & humanities research council (AHRC) Grant Number: AH/D001935/1*. Retrieved from <http://www.northumbria.ac.uk/static/5007/ceispdf/final.pdf> Accessed 1.05.15.

McLeod, J., Childs, S., & Hardiman, R. (2011). Accelerating positive change in electronic records management: Headline findings from a major research project. *Archives and Manuscripts, The Journal of the Australian Society of Archivists*, *39*(2), 65–93.

McLeod, R., & Shipman, A. (2010). Digital preservation and sustainability: Challenges and hurdles, information continuity. *iQ/The R. MAA Quarterly*, *26*(3), 26–28.

Oliver, G. (2004). Investigating information culture: A comparative case study research design and methods. *Archival Science*, *4*, 287–314.

Oliver, G. (2008). Information culture: Exploration of differing values and attitudes to information in organizations. *Journal of Documentation*, *64*(3), 363–385.

Oliver, G. (2011). *Organisational culture for information managers*. Oxford: Chandos Publishing.

Seel, R. (2000). Culture and complexity: New insights on organisational change. *Culture & Complexity-Organisations & People*, *7*(2), 2–9.

Shepherd, E., & Yeo, G. (2003). *Managing Records—A Handbook of Principles and Practice*. London: Facet Publishing.

Svärd, P. (2014). *Information and records management systems and the impact of information culture on the management of public information* (PhD. thesis). University of Amsterdam. Retrieved from <http://dare.uva.nl/document/2/140656> Accessed 20.05.16.

Tieto Corporation. (2013). Information is a strategic business asset—Are you managing it as such? Retrieved from <https://www.tieto.com/sites/default/files/files/information-management-white-paper.pdf> Accessed 25.05.16.

Travica, B. (2008). Information politics and information culture: A case study. *Informing Science Journal*, 211–244.

Widén-Wulff, G. (2000). Business information culture: A qualitative study of the information culture in the Finnish insurance business. *Information Research*, *5*(3). Retrieved from http://informationr.net/ir/5-3/paper77.html (Accessed 7.02.2012).

Wright, T. (2013). Information culture in a government organization: Examining records management training and self-perceived competencies in compliance with a records management program. *Records Management Journal.*, *23*(1), 14–36.

Interview Schedule

The purpose of this interview schedule is to elicit responses regarding information culture in relation to records management in Sundsvall and Härnösand municipalities. (A third case study might be added if permission to carry out research is granted). The questions are directed at different categories of personnel. Information culture and the way it influences records management is an area that has not been explored. In 2010, Douglas defined information culture as: "an emerging complex system of values, attitudes and behaviours that influence how information is used in an organization. Information culture exists in the context of and is influenced by an organizational culture and the wider environment" (Douglas, 2010:388). The data that will be collected will enable me to answer my research questions and hence contribute to a better understanding of how information culture impacts records management. The interview will be 45 minutes long and upon consent of the interviewee, it will be recorded.

According to research on information culture (Oliver, 2011, Douglas, 2010, Choo et al. 2008) attitudes, norms and values impact the way records are handled in an organization. This is what constitutes an information culture espoused by an organization. This research applies Oliver's (2011) framework for assessment of information culture in organizations. The framework constitutes three levels:

Level 1 is the fundamental layer of an organization's culture and among many it includes, respect for information as evidence, respect for information as knowledge, willingness to share information and trust in information.
Level 2 addresses employee skills, knowledge and experience related to information management.
Level 3 is about information governance and trust in organization information systems.

Level One **Respect for records as evidence, Respect for information as knowledge, willingness to share information and Trust in Information.**

1. Is the management of records prioritized and integrated in the business processes? If yes, how is this done?
2. Are there professional staff employed to undertake records management?
3. What function does the records management staff have in the organization? What type of responsibilities do they have and do you have contact with them and if yes, for what?
4. Are you actively informed about the way you should handle public records? If so, is it management or the records professionals? Is this something positive or negative to your work?
5. Do you consider records management to be part of your responsibilities?
6. Are you aware of the laws governing the records that you receive or produce?
7. Do you think these laws are necessary? If yes, explain why.
8. Does the municipality leave up to these laws?
9. Are there common systems to facilitate the use of each other's records?
10. Do you reuse and trust the records?
11. Are there any significant barriers to re-use such as insufficient access to information systems?
12. How do you retrieve records and what retrieval methods do you use?
13. What efforts are put into the effective capture, organization and management of records?
14. Does the municipality have records management systems where records are preserved with metadata?

Level Two **Skills, knowledge and experience related to records management, which can be acquired and/or extended in the workplace:**

1. What is your understanding of records management? What does it involve?
2. Do you receive training in records management?
3. Is training in records management considered important by management?
4. How do you perceive your records management skills to be?
5. How do you think the way you handle records affects they are preserved?
6. What are the consequences of bad records management?
7. Are international standards applied to the management of records in the organization?
8. Does your unit meet to discuss and plan the management of records and is there collaboration among unit members?

Level Three **Records Governance Model and Trust in organizational systems. The records governance model is reflected in the degree of coherence of the overall records architecture (Oliver, 2011).** Oliver makes reference to Davenport's (1997) different information models that can be found in organizations and these include, information federalism, information feudalism, information monarchy, information anarchy and technocratic utopia. **Trust in organizational systems** is about the employees trust in in-house records management systems.

1. How does management deal with records management?
2. Does management expressly demand that you handle public information according to the laws governing it?
3. Is there a records management policy?
4. Are there records management schedules?
5. Are they adhered to?
6. What challenges does the organization face in maintaining records based on best practice.
7. How are records management challenges resolved in the organization?
8. Do you use the information systems put in place to manage records?
9. Are records withheld from systems?

(2012.08.30)

Accountability, transparency, and the role of information management

7

7.1 Introduction

The failure of government institutions to deliver satisfactory services to the citizens resulted in calls for transparency and accountability. Through the different transparency and accountability initiatives, efforts are being made to deepen democracy and increase citizen participation in governance (Joshi, 2013). Transparency and accountability are regarded as tenets of good governance that have emerged to address developmental failures and democratic deficits (Florini, 1999; Rosie McGee & Gaventa, 2011). They are seen as cornerstones of sustainable development. It is believed that true transparency can improve governance and enhance accountability (The International Standards of Supreme Audit Institutions, n.d.). This is why the discourse on transparency and accountability is prioritized on the global agenda and is promoted by both international and nongovernmental organizations. Online and mobile technology tools are also being deployed to promote these two tenets of democracy (Avila, Feigenblatt, Heacock, & Heller, 2010). Harrison and Sayogo (2014), however, contended that information and communication technology (ICT) use to distribute government information (e-transparency) has made the issue of transparency more complex, since it raises technical and privacy issues which could lead to the inadvertent distribution of information and requires the identification of quality information. The disclosure of government information requires resources to deal with the issues that Harisson and Sayogo (2014) highlight.

Transparent and accountable governments promote the well-being of individuals and businesses, which in turn creates prosperous and productive economies. They also enable both political and public institutions to keep an eye on each other and hence hold each other accountable (Bauhr & Grimes, 2014). Transparency is expected to enhance accountability and to induce good behavior in government office holders (Bauhr & Grimes, 2014). Joshi (2013) identified four elements that make up the relationship between power-holders (those voted into power) and the delegator (the citizens). These elements constitute: setting standards, getting information about actions, making judgments about appropriateness, and sanctioning unsatisfactory performance. Transparency and accountability are further seen as enablers of inclusive and sustainable growth and development. Where governments are transparent and accountable, the citizens are empowered to become the drivers of their own development. Budget transparency is a good example of how citizens can be included in the government budgetary process. Therefore, there is a correlation between transparency and the quality of governance that citizens enjoy.

Enterprise Content Management, Records Management and Information Culture Amidst e-Government Development.
DOI: http://dx.doi.org/10.1016/B978-0-08-100874-4.00007-7

According to the World Bank, countries with high levels of budgetary transparency are more democratic and achieve positive development which secures the economic and social rights of their citizens (The World Bank, 2013). Fiscal transparency shows a government's willingness to open up its internal decision-making processes. This gives citizens an opportunity to scrutinize government decisions and to demand action where democracy exists (Harrison & Sayogo, 2014). However, despite this knowledge, millions of people continue to live in countries without accountable and transparent institutions (Sida, 2013). Governments that lack integrity, ethical underpinnings, are corrupt, secretive, and embrace nepotism are not accountable to their citizens and therefore risk losing legitimacy which threatens the stability of societies (Field, 2010). Tabel 7.1 presents principles of good governance as listed by Field:

Table 7.1 Principles of good governance

Legitimacy and voice	– Participation—all men and women should have a voice in decision making, either directly or through legitimate intermediate institutions that represent their intention. Such broad participation is built on freedom of association and speech as well as capacities to participate constructively. – Consensus orientation—good governance mediates differing interests to reach a broad consensus on what is in the best interest of the group and, where possible, on policies and procedures.
Direction	– Strategic vision—leaders and the public have a broad and long-term perspective on good governance and human development, along with a sense of what is needed for such development. There is also an understanding of the historical, cultural, and social complexities in which that perspective is grounded.
Performance responsiveness	– Institutions and processes try to serve all stakeholders. – Effectiveness and efficiency—processes and institutions produce results that meet needs while making the best use of resources.
Accountability	– Decision makers in government, the private sector and civil society organizations are accountable to the public as well as to institutional stakeholders. This accountability differs depending on the organizations and whether the decision is internal or external. – Transparency is built on the free flow of information. Processes, institutions, and information are directly accessible to those concerned with them, and enough information is provided to understand and monitor them.
Fairness and equity	– All men and women have opportunities to improve or maintain their well-being. – Rule of law—legal frameworks should be fair and enforced impartially, particularly the laws on human rights.

7.2 Transparency and accountability

Florini (1999) contended that transparency as a term is loosely defined because it is used in different areas. In politics, the term means providing information to the citizens to enable them to scrutinize the actions of government. She defined transparency as "the release of information by institutions that is relevant to evaluating those institutions" (Florini, 1999, p. 5). Johnston, Gary, and David (2005, p. 2) presented transparency as, "official business conducted in such a way that substantive and procedural information is available to, and broadly understandable by, people and groups in society, subject to reasonable limits protecting security and privacy." Joshi (2013, p. 31) defined transparency initiatives as, "any attempts (by states or citizens) to place information or processes that were previously opaque in the public domain, accessible for use by citizen groups or policy-makers." Graham, Amos, Plumptre (2003) posited that transparency is deeply rooted in the principles of good governance which include some principles discussed in Tabel 7.1.

Transparency is closely connected to accountability because, through the information that is made available to the citizens, those in power are called upon to account for their actions. Accountability refers to the legal reporting framework, organizational structures, strategy, procedures and actions (The International Standards of Supreme Audit Institutions, n.d.). Iacovino (2010, p. 181) defined accountability as, "synonymous with transparency, openness, trust and responsibility, as opposed to secrecy, cover-up, and corruption." Stapenhurst (n.d., p. 1) offered the definition of accountability as "an amorphous concept that is difficult to define in precise terms." However, broadly speaking, accountability exists when there is a relationship where an individual or body, and the performance of tasks or functions by that individual or body, are subject to another's oversight, direction or request that they provide information or justification for their actions. McGee *et al.* (2010, p. 4) quoted Tisné (2010, p. 2) who defined accountability as, "the process of holding actors responsible for their actions. More specifically, it is the concept that individuals, agencies and organizations (public, private and civil society) are held responsible for executing their powers according to a certain standard (whether set mutually or not)." Borowiak (2011, p. 1) used the term "democratic accountability" as "a sovereign national community of citizens who delegate governing authority to public officials. As an expression of their ultimate authority, these citizens then hold those officials to account for how well they have carried out their governing responsibilities." Accountability is globally viewed as a standard of political legitimacy. Its opposite, nonaccountability, is a measure of dysfunction. Accountability has an ethical dimension and cannot be entirely legislated (Iacovino, 2010).

7.3 Access to government information

One of the most important instruments of citizens' control of public authorities is the principle of public access to official records, that is, information generated by public institutions in conduct of their business. The governing principles of access to information are transparency, active participation, responsiveness, and accountability (UNDP, 2013, p. 2). The information age has meant an increased supply of and demand for information. Advancements in technology have made the publication of government information easier, which has in turn raised the citizens' expectations about transparency and accountability. Freedom of information is part and parcel of an effective and democratic government (Mulley, 2010). The free flow of information from the government to the citizens is crucial to good governance because it is informed citizens that can hold their governments accountable for the policies and decisions they make on their behalf. Access to information further strengthens the conditions for transparency and accountability. It is also a basis for efficiency within government institutions and facilitates decision-making processes (Sida, 2013). The right to access information is recognized as a fundamental democratic right in Article 19 of the United Nations Universal Declaration of Human Rights (Fox, 2010). This right is further guaranteed through national constitutions in countries where freedom of information laws (FOI) have been adopted. FOI laws are recognized as international laws and they allow citizens to protect their rights, and are a safeguard against abuses, mismanagement, and corruption (Banisar, 2006). Citizens need to access vital information on issues that affect their lives such as health, weather, education, culture, and politics to name but a few. Official information is, therefore, of extreme importance and should be of good quality that is; complete, reliable, authentic, and trustworthy.

Bamgbose and Etim (2015, p. 1) argued that, "Information is the stimulus of all the thoughts and actions of living creatures. No doubt, it is a prerequisite for the functioning of the modern society because success in every area of human endeavour is premised on its intelligent use." Democracy building requires knowledgeable citizens who can act on their rights. Recorded information enables citizens to access their constitutional rights and reliable and trustworthy information is crucial to the delivery of public services (Abuzawayda, Zawiyah, & Aziz, 2012). The role of records management in government institutions is, therefore, to identify and manage records for accountability (Johnson, 2003). Records are evidence of experiences and human activities and they enhance memory (Cunningham, 2005, p. 22). The aggregation of government records is what makes up government archives and in democratic societies, archives are meant to enhance democratic transparency and accountability. They empower members of the communities where there is access. That way, communities can monitor those they vote into power and influence bad governance, corruption, and lack of accountability (Cunningham, 2005:24). In established democracies such as in the Scandinavian countries, government archives and the national archives play a major role in enhancing transparency and accountability (Gränström, Lundquist, & Fredriksson, 2000; Jørgensen, 2014). Government information is released in two forms: proactively, whereby government institutions publish what is now known as open data on their websites, and demand driven release of information which builds on the citizens' requests for information (Jeffison & Lujala, 2015).

In fledgling democracies where transparency and accountability is still low, archives and archival institutions are neglected and hardly have the resources to play their role as the guardians and custodians of government information (International Records Management Trust, 2008; Svärd, 2008, 2013). Since all governments are participating in the information age, the effective management of government information is of paramount importance to long-term transparency and accountability. The digital environment requires robust information and records management regimes and information management systems. In the digital and networked environment, the management of government information has become crucial since it is sometimes hard to establish the provenance of information and hence the responsibility for its management. Iacovino (2010) contended that memory loss in the electronic world is a threat to accountability. The networked digital environment has increased the complexity and volume of information that government institutions have to effectively manage in order to enhance their open governance structure. Thurston (2015) argued that building high-quality evidence involves an interface between interconnected laws, standards, well-defined metadata architectures, and technology systems. Archival legislation is, e.g., meant to enhance the effective management of government information and to promote access. In Sweden, the Archival Law requires all government institutions to manage their information/records in a manner that promotes readily access to information (Bohlin, 2010; Gränström et al., 2000). The Archival Law is, however, usually only known to archivists and registrars and yet it is the basis for the effective management of government information and therefore key to safe guarding citizens' rights (Svärd, 2011, 2014).

Information can only be accessed where there are structures to capture and manage it for dissemination, preservation, and reuse. Poor information management regimes prevent access to information. Though transparency and accountability hinge on access to information, issues regarding its management are not equally prioritized especially in developing countries with poor information management infrastructures (Abuzawayda et al., 2012; Kemoni & Ngulube, 2008; Ngoepe, 2004). Mutula and Wamukoya (2009) postulated that sound information management is the basis for democratic governance. As democracy and good governance take momentum in, e.g., the developing countries, the key challenge that remains to be addressed is the role of information in promoting democracy, transparency, accountability, and the integrity in government. Today's most prominent trend is the push for governments to release their data in order to increase accountability and transparency. This type of information is referred to as open data (Kalathil, 2015). The dissemination of government information additionally requires the use of different information technologies and other mechanisms, such as print media, radio, talk shows, and chalkboards to disseminate information to communities that still lack well diffused and developed Internet connectivity and with low literacy levels (Kalathil, 2015; Teemu, 2013).

7.4 Promoting transparency and accountability

There are discernible efforts that are globally being undertaken to promote transparency and accountability. We are witnessing the creation of multistakeholder and citizen-led approaches because in, e.g., African countries, traditional accountability measures, such as internal audits or intra-government controls, are no longer considered sufficient due to corruption (McGee et al., 2010). Global transparency and accountability efforts include but are not only limited to; e-Government development initiatives which are expected to create more effective, transparent and accountable and inclusive institutions; The European Public Sector Information directive which requires all European governments to release public sector information to the public for further use and the development of new electronic services (The European Union, 2003); The Global Open Data Initiative which was launched in 2013, and aims to globally champion open data for enhanced transparency and accountability; effective service delivery, and economic growth (Alonso, 2013); The Open Governance Partnership (OGP) initiative that was established in 2011 and has 70 participating members — it promotes partnership between nations and their civil society organizations with an aim of effecting reforms at a national level. It is also a partnership between nations and enhances collaboration and the sharing of good ideas and practices on issues of transparency, integrity, and public safety. The OGP goals of increased transparency, accountability and engagement seek to: (a) improve public services; (b) improve public integrity; (c) more effectively manage public resources; (d) create safer communities; and (e) increase corporate accountability (Macaulay, 2014). Admission to the OGP requires countries to have a legal basis that promotes access to information by the citizens (Harrison & Sayogo, 2014).

The Global Initiative for Fiscal Transparency was launched in 2011 with the objective to promote fiscal transparency, engagement, and accountability in countries around the world (International Budget Partnership, 2011), The International Aid Transparency Initiative was launched in 2008 with an aim of making information about aid spending easier to access, use and understand (International Aid Transparency Initiative, n.d.), The Open Contracting and the Extractive Industries Transparency Initiate were launched in 2002 at the World Summit on Sustainable Development — it has the aim to improve the management of natural resources, reduce corruption, and mitigate conflict (Haufler, 2010). Though there is a global push for transparency and accountability as demonstrated above, it is not all the citizens of the globe that are enjoying the fruits of these global initiatives. Gaventa and McGee (2013) and Joshi (2013) contended that the available evidence on the impact of transparency and accountability initiatives is fragmented and limited. A good example of how government transparency and accountability initiatives can fail citizens is demonstrated in the efforts to rebuild post-conflict societies through the establishment of Truth and Reconciliation Commissions (TRCs) as the section below demonstrates.

7.5 Addressing past harms in postconflict societies

Transparency and accountability is further of key importance when addressing past harms in post-conflict countries. A number of post-conflict countries have embraced transitional justice instruments, such as Truth and Reconciliation Commissions (TRCs) to address the past of human rights violations. TRCs are temporary institutions that are set up to investigate and document human rights abuses in a particular country (Brahm, 2007; Hayner, 2002). They are often sanctioned by national governments (Brahm, 2005). Post-conflict governments have to account for the past wrongs in order to forge a democratic future. Peterson (2005, p. 2) posited that "the purpose of a truth commission is to break through that wall of silence and restore knowledge of the hitherto hidden hands in history." It is believed, that acknowledging the past, which in the case of TRCs has meant giving victims and perpetrators a platform to recount their war experiences, is supposed to bring about healing and reconciliation. Reconciliation is about mending broken relationships and the aim of TRCs is to prevent further violence and future human rights abuses (Hayner, 2002). Genuine reconciliation, however, builds on the truth and full disclosure which is achieved through the investigative work of the TRCs and which includes the documentation of the committed atrocities. Wilson (2004, p. 5) argued that "individuals, minorities and societies cannot achieve justice, validate their rights and carry through their efforts for reconciliation, unless the authoritative evidence of the violations which they have suffered is preserved and accessible." The results of the TRC work is supposed to lead to the development of a new society that builds on democratic values which should include access to information.

Therefore, the documentation that TRCs create captures memories of societies, and it is a historical record of the committed atrocities. This history should be optimally used as post-conflict countries forge their future (Bakiner, 2014). Peterson identified three types of records that TRCs create and these include: administrative records, such as personnel records, program records which document the work of the commission, and investigative records on individuals or incidents. The investigative records may constitute: video clips, databases, audiotapes, digital as well as paper records, and photographs. Based on the accumulated documentation, TRCs come up with a final report which is supposed to be widely disseminated to the people but which rarely happens (Svärd, 2007, 2009, 2013). TRCs do a commendable job and their rich documentation clarifies the relation between violations of civil and political rights, economic, social, and cultural rights. Based on this rich documentation, they often come up with recommendations for institutional reforms that aim to create a legal, political, and cultural framework that builds on peace and democracy (Bakiner, 2014). Postconflict governments are expected to honor these recommendations but that is not often the case (Svärd, 2010). The TRC documentation is meant to educate the citizens about the causes of the conflicts to avoid regression. TRCs that have taken place in countries with poor information management infrastructures have failed to effectively use this accumulated documentation for the benefit of the traumatized and impoverished people (Svärd, 2009, 2010). This documentation can only be of value if it can be used in a manner that generates new knowledge and understanding. Knowledge about human rights abuses is important and the truth that TRCs establish has to be accessible to the public.

The Liberian TRC is a good example of what happens where there is lack of information planning and a well-developed information management infrastructure. The TRC collected over 22,000 written statements, several dozen personal interviews, and more than 500 live public testimonies of witnesses, including both perpetrators of atrocities and direct victims, in 15 counties and the Liberian Diaspora. This documentation constitutes records that need a secure and trustworthy custodianship, where access should be steered through fair rules to protect the privacy of the names of the people that are named in the archives (Peterson, 2005). These conditions were nonexistent and the controversies that the TRC report caused made the Liberian TRC to entrust all its documentation (archives) to the Georgia Institute of Technology in Atlanta. This might have been an attempt to safeguard the archives since the commission recommended that the incumbent president of Liberia and some of the perpetrators of the conflict who are now in power should step down and leave government offices and politics. This is the first time in history a sovereign state handed over its entire TRC documentation to a foreign power (Svärd, 2013). This documentation however belongs to the Liberian people and it is their intellectual property. Governments are responsible for the information that is generated as a result of their activities. Since the TRC was sanctioned by the Liberian government, it is its responsibility to safeguard the TRC archives, manage, preserve, and to make them accessible to the citizens and hence respect the victims' right to know. The TRC archives are important for democracy building, transparency and accountability, reconciliation, research purposes, enhancing knowledge about conflicts and for posterity.

To enhance reconciliation, the causes of the conflict have to be addressed to enable people to engage in the reconstruction of their societies and to establish decent lives. The TRC archives carry the evidentiary value upon which the victims of oppression can base their claims for reparations and for all the Liberian citizens to demand the implementation of the TRC recommendations. Access to the TRC records in some countries is limited and yet it might be the only qualifier for reparations. Reparations are a central issue to the reconciliation process and a risk of not being paid out where there is no pressure exerted on the government by the public or civil society groups. As countries continue to embrace TRCs as mechanisms of transitional justice, the people whose atrocities they document continue to suffer since the TRC recommendations are not honored and the reparations are not paid out to all victims (Svärd, 2010). The plight of the poor continues because change in their lives never takes place (Laplante & Theidon, 2007; Sesay, 2007). Populations emerging from experiences of repression have expectations such as justice for victims, accelerated economic recovery and development through the creation of inclusive and accountable institutions. Therefore, people need to know about the TRC findings in order to claim their rights. Reconciliation is a gradual process and for it to take place; the causes of the conflict have to be addressed.

Post-conflict countries such as Liberia lack access to technology and proper institutions to effectively use the generated information. In August, 2016, the author visited the Independent Human Rights Commission of Liberia that is supposed to further the work of the TRC and to see to it that the government honors and implements its recommendations. It was supposed to have taken over the TRC archives and to manage them. A conversation with one of the officers revealed that the Commission does not have access to the TRC archives. The Commission for obvious purposes needs a copy of these archives for its work. TRC archives form a collective memory, and are cultural heritage of the countries that use them as transitional justice mechanisms. The archives should be well maintained in order to preserve their integrity and authenticity especially now with the developing sphere of disinformation.

A well-functioning information management infrastructure should be put in place at the commencement of each TRC mission to effectively capture, manage, disseminate, and to preserve the TRC archives in a manner that would lead to their use. The preservation of the documentation on war atrocities has to be budgeted for during the early phases of the TRC work. Where there is danger for destruction, a copy of the archives should be secured and preserved at institutions that are considered safer, outside the country in question. It is of crucial importance that a copy of the archives is retained in the country for the legitimacy of the TRC process. The TRC archives are a collective memory and an information bank that should educate present and future generations about the causes of violence and thereby prevent a repetition of the same mistakes. They, therefore, enhance transparency and accountability should they be used intelligently. The TRC case demonstrates the importance of information management to the reconstruction of post-conflict societies and the promotion of transparency, accountability and sustainable development. Post-conflict governments account for human rights violations by sanctioning the establishment of transitional justice mechanisms such as TRCS.

7.6 Conclusion

Transparency and accountability are globally considered essential to good governance. It is transparent and accountable governments that promote democracy and sustainable development through inclusive and efficient institutions that are able to deliver quality services to the citizens. Despite this knowledge, many citizens of the world still live in countries with governments that are not transparent and accountable to them and hence with high levels of corruption. This deprives the poor of any development possibilities and hinders the free flow of information which is crucial to holding government officials accountable for the decisions they make on behalf of the citizens. According to the literature reviewed, there is a clear correlation between effective information management and transparency and accountability. Nevertheless, what is often left out in the discussions on transparency and accountability is the importance of a well-developed information management infrastructure that is supposed to facilitate the documentation of government actions and facilitate access to government information. What is crucial to all the reporting systems required by the mentioned transparency and accountability initiatives is trustworthy and understandable information. This requires information systems that are reliable and that enable the effective creation, capture, organization, management, dissemination and preservation for reuse of government information (Svärd, 2014).

Developing countries still lack robust information management regimes and systems, which are supposed to ensure that government information is well-captured and managed for further dissemination and for governance purposes. This hinders readily access to government information and obstructs the objectives of transparency and accountability. The networked society requires laws, standards, well-defined metadata architectures, and information management systems. Developing countries will therefore have to harness information technology to reap the benefits of open data and to make it available to interested citizens. Lack of investments in information planning and robust information infrastructures and the political will led to the expatriation of the entire Liberian TRC archives. This was not fair to the victims who contributed with their narrations despite the trauma that they had to recount. They ought to benefit from the use of the archives together with the rest of the Liberian society. Reconciliation is a long-term process and can take generations which confirms the crucial importance of the TRC archives in promoting an understanding of the causes of conflict and preventing regression to conflict. The effectiveness of TRCs as instruments of transitional justice will only be achieved if the recommendations they make are honored and implemented by the respective governments. This makes the dissemination of the information they generate of paramount importance, if the citizens are to be made aware of their rights to reparations and if they are to demand the implementation of the recommendations. TRCs are impartial instruments that address past harms and promote transparency and accountability by excavating the truth, but the information they generate needs to be prioritized and used in order to promote transitional justice.

References

Abuzawayda, Y.I., Zawiyah, M.Y., & Aziz, M.J.A. (2012). *International Journal of Information Technology & Computer Science, Vol 5* (Issue on September/October), pp. 1–7.

Alonso, M.J. (2013). Announcing the Global Open Data Initiative (GODI). Retrieved from <http://webfoundation.org/2013/06/announcing-the-global-open-data-initiative-godi/> (accessed 21 July 2016).

Avila, R., Feigenblatt, H., Heacock, R. & Heller, N. (2010). Global Mapping of Technology for Transparency and Accountability. New technologies. Retrieved from <http://www.transparency-initiative.org/wp-content/uploads/2011/05/global_mapping_of_technology_final1.pdf> (accessed 20 July 2016).

Bakiner, O. (2014). Truth Commission Impact: An Assessment of How Commissions Influence Politics and Society. *International Journal of Transitional Justice*, *8*(1), 6–30.

Bamgbose, O.J. & Etim, I.A. (2015). Accessing Government Information in Africa through the Right to Know: The Role of the Library. Retrieved from <http://library.ifla.org/1221/1/114-bamgbose-en.pdf> (accessed 15 April 2016).

Banisar, D. (2006). *Freedom of Information Around the World 2006. A Global Survey of Access to Government Information Laws*. Retrieved from <http://www.humanrightsinitiative.org/programs/ai/rti/international/laws_papers/intl/global_foi_survey_2006.pdf> (accessed 15 April 2016).

Bauhr, M., & Grimes, M. (2014). Indignation or Resignation: The Implications of Transparency for Societal Accountability. *Governance: An International Journal of Policy, Administration, and Institutions*, *27*(2), 291–320.

Bohlin, A. (2010). In Åttonde Upplaga (Ed.), *Offentlighetsprincipen*. Mölnlycke: Elanders Sverige AB.

Borowiak, C.T. (2011). *Accountability and Democracy: The Pitfalls and Promise of Popular Control* Retrieved from <http://www.oxfordscholarship.com.till.biblextern.sh.se/view/10.1093/acprof:oso/9780199778256.001.0001/acprof-9780199778256-chapter-0> (accessed 11 July 2016).

Brahm, E. (2005). *Getting to the Bottom of Truth: Examining Truth Commission Success and Impact*. Paper presented at the International Studies Association Annual Meeting, Honolulu, Hawaii. <http://center.theparentscircle.org/images/252391 51e8cf4a29a2f3046308307f4a.pdf> (accessed 12 July 2016).

Brahm, E. (2007). Uncovering the Truth: Examining Truth Commission Success and Impact. *International Studies Perspectives*, *8*, 16–35, accessed 28 July 2016.

Field, C. (2010). Promoting Accountable and Transparent Decision Making in the Public Sector. Retrieved from <http://www.ombudsman.wa.gov.au/Publications/Documents/speeches/030610-Speech-by-Chris-Field-to-Legal-Wise-Conference-2010.pdf> (accessed 16 July 2016).

Florini, A. (1999). Does the Invisible Hand Need a Transparent Glove? The Politics of Transparency. Retrieved from <http://siteresources.worldbank.org/INTWBIGOVANTCOR/Resources/florini.pdf> (accessed 20 April 2016).

Fox, J. (2010). The Uncertain Relationship Between Transparency and Accountability. *Development in Practice*, *17*(Numbers 4–5), 663–671.

Gaventa, J., & McGee, R. (2013). The Impact of Transparency and Accountability Initiatives. *Development Policy Review*, *31*(S1), 3–28.

Graham, J., Amos, B. & Plumptre, T. (2003). Principles for Good Governance in the 21st Century. Policy Brief No.15. Retrieved from <http://unpan1.un.org/intradoc/groups/public/documents/UNPAN/UNPAN011842.pdf> (accessed 10 July 2016).

Gränström, C., Lundquist, L., & Fredriksson, K. (2000). *Arkivlagen, Bakgrund och kommentarer*. Göteborg: Graphic Systems AB, (Vol. andra upplagan,).

Harrison, T. M., & Sayogo, D. S. (2014). Transparency, Participation, and Accountability Practices in Open Government: A Comparative Study. *Government Information Quarterly*, *31*, 513–525.

Haufler, V. (2010). Disclosure as Governance: The Extractive Industries Transparency Initiative and Resource Management in the Developing World. *Global Environmental Politics*, *10*(3), 53–73.

Hayner, P. (2002). *Unspeakable Truths: Confronting State Terror and Atrocity by Priscilla B. Hayner*. New York: Routledge.

Iacovino, L. (2010). Archives as Arsenals of Accountability. In Currents of Archival. In Thinking (Ed.), *Eastwood Terry and MacNeil, Heather*. Santa Barbara: CA: Libraries Unlimited.

International Aid Transparency Initiative. (n.d.). Supporting Aid Transparency. Retrieved from <http://www.publishwhatyoufund.org/files/IATI-brochure.pdf> (accessed 18 July, 2016).

International Budget Partnership. (2011). A Global Initiative on Fiscal Transparency, Engagement and Accountability. Retrieved from <http://www.internationalbudget.org/2011/07/launch-of-gift-global-initiative-on-fiscal-transparency-engagement-and-accountability/> (accessed 18 July 2016).

International Records Management Trust. (2008). Sierra Leone Case Study. Fostering Trust and Transparency in Governance. Investigating and Addressing the Requirements for Building Integrity in Public Sector Information Systems in the ICT Environment.

Retrieved from <http://www.irmt.org/documents/building_integrity/case_studies/IRMT_Case_Study_Sierra%20Leone.pdf> (accessed 20 April 2015).

Jeffison, Y., Ofori, J., & Lujala, P. (2015). Illusionary Transparency? Oil Revenues, Information Disclosure, and Transparency. *Society & Natural Resources*, *28*, 1187–1202.

The Relevance of Archival Practice within "E-Democracy." In C. Johnson *Political Pressure and the Archival Record.* Chicago: The Society of American Archivists.

Johnston, P., Gary, B. V., & David, V. (2005). The Benefits of Electronic Records Management Systems. A General Review of Published and Some Unpublished Cases. *Records Management Journal*, *15*(3), 131–140.

Joshi, A. (2013). Do They Work? Assessing the Impact of Transparency and Accountability Initiatives in Service Delivery. *Development Policy Review*, *31*(S1), 29–48. Retrieved from <http://r4d.dfid.gov.uk/PDF/Outputs/Mis_SPC/60827_DPRJoshi_Preprint.pdf> (accessed 20 July 2016).

Jørgensen, O. (2014). Access to Information in the Nordic Countries. A comparison of the laws of Sweden, Finland, Denmark, Norway and Iceland and International Rules. Retrieved from <http://www.nordicom.gu.se/sites/default/files/publikationer-hela-pdf/access_to_information_in_the_nordic_countries_2014_0.pdf> (accessed 25 July 2016).

Kalathil, S. (2015). Transparency, Accountability and Technology. Retrieved from <https://www.planusa.org/docs/ict-accountability-2015.pdf> (accessed 9 July 2016).

Kemoni, H., & Ngulube, P. (2008). Relationship between Records Management, Public Service Delivery and the Attainment of the United Nations Millennium Development Goals in Kenya. *Information Development*, *24*(4), 296–305.

Laplante, L. J., & Theidon, K. (2007). Truth with Consequences: Justice and Reparations in Post-Truth Commission Peru. *Human Rights Quarterly*, *29*, 228–250.

Macaulay, M. (2014). The Open Government Partnership: What Are the Challenges and Opportunities for New Zealand? Retrieved from <http://ndhadeliver.natlib.govt.nz/delivery/DeliveryManagerServlet?dps_pid = IE20421806> (accessed 21 July 2016).

McGee, R. & Gaventa, J. (2011). Shifting Power? Assessing the Impact of Transparency and Accountability Initiatives. <http://www.ids.ac.uk/publication/shifting-power-assessing-the-impact-of-transparency-and-accountability-initiatives> (accessed 11 April 2016).

McGee, R., Gaventa, J., Barrett, G., Calland, R., Carlitz, R., Joshi, A. & Acosta, A.M. (2010). The Impact and Effectiveness of Transparency and Accountability Initiatives: A Review of the Evidence to Date. Synthesis Report. Retrieved from <http://citeseerx.ist.psu.edu/viewdoc/download?doi = 10.1.1.475.4323&rep = rep1&type = pdf> (accessed 9 April 2016).

Mulley, S. (2010). Donor Aid. New Frontiers in Transparency and Accountability. Retrieved from <http://transparencyinitiative.theideabureau.netdna-cdn.com/wp-content/uploads/2011/05/donor_aid_final1.pdf> (accessed 20 July 2016).

Mutula, S., & Wamukoya, J. M. (2009). Public Sector Information Management in East and Southern Africa: Implications for FOI, Democracy and Integrity in Government. *International Journal of Information Management*, *29*, 333–341.

Ngoepe, M. (2004). Accountability, Transparency and Good Governance: The National Archives and Records Service of South Africa's Role in Helping Government to Better Service Delivery to the South Africans. Paper presented at the Library and Information Association of South Africa, South Africa. <https://www.researchgate.net/publication/274952383_Accountability_transparency_and_good_governance_the_National_Archives_and_Records_Service_of_South_Africa's_role_in_helping_government_to_better_service_delivery_to_the_South_Africans> (accessed 19 April 2016).

Peterson, H.T. (2005). *Final Acts. A Guide to Preserving the Records of Truth Commissions.* Retrieved from <https://www.wilsoncenter.org/sites/default/files/Petersonfinpdf.pdf> (accessed 27 July 2016).

Sesay, A. (2007). *Does One Size Fit All? The Sierra Leone Truth and Reconciliation Commission revisited.* Stockholm: Elanders Gotab AB, Vol. Discussion Paper 36.

Sida. (2013). Accountability, Transparency and the Rule of Law as Drivers for Inclusive Growth and Development. Retrieved from <http://www.sida.se/contentassets/4f1d61e6026746b4a76c74390e7b6dd9/background-paper-on-transparency-accountability-and-rol.pdf> (accessed 20 July 2016).

Stapenhurst, R. (n.d.). Accountability in Governance. Retrieved from <http://siteresources.worldbank.org/PUBLICSECTORANDGOVERNANCE/Resources/AccountabilityGovernance.pdf> (accessed 18 July 2016).

Svärd, P. (2007). The Challenges of Documenting War Atrocities in Post-Conflict Sierra Leone: A Study of the Truth and Reconciliation Commission (TRC). *African Journal of International Affairs (AJIA), 10*, 55–72.

Svärd, P. (2008). The Role of Archives in Enhancing Accountability and Transparency—The Case of Sierra Leone. *Journal of the Eastern and Southern Africa Regional Branch of the International Council on Archives, 27*, 20–38.

Svärd, P. (2009). Access and Democratisation of Information: The Documentation of War Atrocities by the Liberian Truth and Reconciliation Commission. *Comma, 2008*(1), 123–134.

Svärd, P. (2010). The International Community and Post-War Reconciliation in Africa: A Case Study of the Sierra Leone Truth and Reconciliation Commission. *African Journal on Conflict Resolution, 10*(1), 35–62.

Svärd, P. (2011). *The Interface between Enterprise Content Management and Records Management in Changing Organizations. (Licentiate Degree)* (p. 71). Härnösand: Mid Sweden University.

Svärd, P. (2013). Liberia's Truth and Reconciliation Commission: The Importance of Documentation in Postwar Education and Reconciliation. Retrieved from <http://forums.ssrc.org/kujenga-amani/author/proscovia-svard/> (accessed 28 July 2016).

Svärd, P. (2014). *Information and Records Management Systems and the Impact of Information Culture on the Management of Public Information. (PhD Degree).* Amsterdam: University of Amsterdam.

Teemu. (2013). Open Government and Freedom of Information in Liberia—More Than a Hollywood Dream? Retrieved from <http://ilabliberia.org/2013/09/29/open-government-and-freedom-of-information-in-liberia-more-than-hollywood-dream/> (accessed 20 April 2016).

The European Union. (2003). Directive 2003/98/EC of the European Parliament and of the Council of 17 November 2003 on the Re-use of Public Sector Information. *Official Journal of the European Union. L 345, pp. 0090–0096.*

The International Standards of Supreme Audit Institutions, I. (n.d.). Principles of Transparency and Accountability. Retrieved from <http://www.issai.org/media/12930/issai_20_e_.pdf> (accessed 12 July 2016).

The World Bank. (2013). Global Stock-Take of Social Accountability Initiatives for Budget Transparency and Monitoring, Key Challenges and Lessons Learned. Retrieved from <http://siteresources.worldbank.org/EXTSOCIALDEVELOPMENT/Resources/244362-1193949504055/4348035-1380737852287/BTM_Stocktake_Report_Final.pdf> (accessed 20 April 2016).

Thurston, A. (2015). Managing Records and Information for Transparent, Accountable and Inclusive Governance in the Digital Environment. Lessons from Nordic Countries. Retrieved from <http://www.irmt.org/wp2/wp-content/uploads/2015/07/Right-to-Information-Lessons-from-Nordic-Countries.pdf> (accessed 20 July 2016).

UNDP. (2013). Access to Information. Retrieved from <http://www.undp.org/content/dam/aplaws/publication/en/publications/democratic-governance/dg-publications-for-website/access-to-information-practice-note/A2I_PN_English.pdf> (accessed 20 July 2016).

Wilson, E. I. (2004). Foreword in Comma. *Comma, International Journal on Archives*, 2, 5.

Index

Note: Page numbers followed by "*f*" and "*t*" refer to figures and tables, respectively.

Kolibri 360 GmbH
Ferdinand-Jühlke-Straße 7
99095 Erfurt, Deutschland
produktsicherheit@kolibri360.de